Geography in the Early Years

The presence of geography in the National Curriculum in England and Wales means that even teachers of children in the first years of school need to consider and monitor the distinctively geographical element in their teaching. Joy Palmer here helps them to do so enjoyably, combining concise summaries of the latest research with transcripts of classroom conversation, case studies and suggestions for the development and implementation of sound geographical work in practice. A final section provides a brief guide to resources available to the teacher.

Joy Palmer is Senior Lecturer in Education at the University of Durham. Recent publications include *Environmental Education in the Primary School* and *The Handbook of Environmental Education*.

Teaching and Learning in the First Three Years of School
Series Editor *Joy Palmer*

This innovatory and up-to-date series is concerned specifically with curriculum practice in the first three years of school. Each book includes
guidance on:

- subject content
- planning and organisation
- assessment and record-keeping
- in-service training

This practical advice is placed in the context of the National Curriculum
and the latest theoretical work on how children learn at this age and what
experiences they bring to their early years in the classroom.

Geography in the Early Years

Joy Palmer

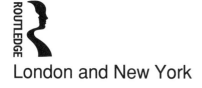

London and New York

First published 1994
by Routledge
11 New Fetter Lane, London EC4P 4EE

Simultaneously published in the USA and Canada
by Routledge
29 West 35th Street, New York, NY 10001

© 1994 Joy Palmer

Typeset in Palatino by Michael Mepham, Frome, Somerset
Printed and bound in Great Britain by
Biddles Ltd, Guildford and King's Lynn
Printed on acid free paper

British Library Cataloguing in Publication Data
A catalogue record for this book is available from the
British Library

Library of Congress Cataloging-in-Publication Data
Palmer, Joy.
  Geography in the early years/Joy Palmer.
  p. cm. – (Teaching and learning in the first three
  years of school)
  Includes bibliographical references and index.
  1. Geography – Study and teaching (Elementary)
  I. Title. II. Series.
  G73.P235   1994
  372.89′1–dc20   93–41050
                                                         CIP

ISBN 0–415–09830–0

Contents

Illustrations

TABLES

Editor's preface

Each book in this series focuses on a specific curriculum area. The series relates relevant learning theory or a rationale for early years learning to the practical development and implementation of subject-based topics and classroom activities at the infant level (i.e. Reception, Y1, Y2). It seems that the majority of existing books on primary education and the primary curriculum focus on pupils aged 7–11 years. It is hoped that this series presents a refreshing and much needed change in that it specifically addresses the first three years in school.

Each volume is intended to be an up-to-date, judicious mix of theory and practical classroom application, offering a wealth of background information, ideas and advice to all concerned with planning, implementing, monitoring and evaluating teaching and learning in the first three years in school. Theoretical perspectives are presented in a lively and interesting way, drawing upon recent classroom research findings wherever possible. Case studies and activities from a range of classrooms and schools illuminate many of the substantial issues related to the subject area in question.

Readers will find a similar pattern of contents in all the books in the series. Each discusses the early learning environment, transition from home- to school-based learning, and addresses the key questions of what this means for the early years teacher and the curriculum. Such discussion inevitably incorporates ideas on the knowledge which young children may have of subjects and an overview of the subject matter itself which is under scrutiny. As the thrust of the series is towards young children learning subjects, albeit in a holistic way, no doubt readers will wish to consider what is an appropriate content or rationale for the subject in the early years. Having considered young children as learners, what they are bringing into school in terms of prior knowledge, the teacher's task and the subject matter itself, each book then turns its attention to appropriate methods of planning, organising, implementing and evaluating teaching and learning activities. Crucial matters such as assessment, evaluation and record-keeping are dealt with in their own right, and are also referred to and discussed in ongoing examples of good practice. Each book concludes with useful suggestions for further staffroom discussion/INSET activities and advice on resources.

As a whole, the series aims to be inspirational and forward-looking. As all readers know so well, the National Curriculum is not 'written in concrete'. Education is a dynamic process. While taking due account of the essential National Curriculum framework, authors go far beyond the level of description of rigid content guidelines to highlight *principles* for teaching and learning. Furthermore, they incorporate two key messages which surely underpin successful, reflective education, namely 'vision' and 'enthusiasm'. It is hoped that students and teachers will be inspired and assisted in their task of implementing successful and progressive plans which help young learners to make sense of their world and the key areas of knowledge within it.

Joy A. Palmer

Acknowledgements

The author gratefully acknowledges the advice and support received from many individuals and schools. In particular, thanks are due to Carole Goodchild (Head Teacher), Alison Ashton (Deputy Head) and Joy King Lane (school co-ordinator for geography and Key Stage 1 consultant for geography in Cleveland) for the case study 'Organising geographical education: a whole-school approach' (Newtown Infant School), for their contribution of ideas for resources, and for the two children's recording sheets included in Chapter 5; also to Imogen Berisford for the case study 'The use of story', and to Ms Brockband and the staff of St Patrick's RC Primary School, Wigan, for the case study 'Developing and using the school grounds in the early years'.

Chapter 1

The young child in the geographical world

INTRODUCTION

The National Curriculum Order for Geography provides a much needed rationale for teaching and learning in this subject area, and addresses a number of fundamental criticisms which have been directed at teaching and learning in geography; notably the lack of attention that has been paid in schools to the distinctive contribution that geography can make to children's learning, and the traditional limitations of study in this area. From the outset, however, it must be emphasised that while National Curriculum documentation for the early years is obviously referred to and incorporated in the forthcoming pages, this volume discusses general principles of teaching and learning in geographical education applicable to all 'early years' children of school age, that is, in the first three years in school.

It is considered a difficult, if not inappropriate, task to pursue any discussion of learning experiences relating to the subject matter of geography in the early years of schooling without also making reference to the cross-curricular theme of environmental education. These two curriculum components are to a large extent inextricably linked in the work of Reception classes and throughout the infant school; therefore their inter-relationships are considered, and practical examples throughout the book take account of teaching and learning across the whole spectrum of geography and what might be termed 'environmental geography'.

The chief aim of this volume is to provide a text which is interesting, illuminative and, above all, helpful to teachers who are going about the complex task of developing worthwhile geographical education for children in the first three years in school.

Essentially it sets about providing an overview of some of the more theoretical aspects of early years learning in geography, illuminated by up-to-date research findings; and illustrates these with discussion, case studies and suggestions for the development and implementation of sound geographical work in practice. It is intended, therefore, to be a judicious mix of theory and practice, enlivened throughout by practical examples deriving from a wide range of schools and classrooms.

Beyond a consideration of theoretical perspectives on learning and links between the subject matter of geography and environment education the text considers the critical topics of organisation and planning, assessment, record-keeping, resources and activities for in-service training meetings.

While geography in the first three years in school is inevitably planned at the level of whole-school policy and approach, and implemented with class or year groups, the individual child is inevitably at the heart of the learning process. Each child has a unique relationship with the world in which he or she is growing up: a relationship based on feelings, experiences and interactions with people, places, objects and events. It is hoped that this focus on 'the young child in the geographical world' extends beyond the heading for the book's opening chapter, and permeates readers' reflections on the text in its entirety.

It seems, therefore, only appropriate that the opening words of text set the scene by focusing on what young learners actually do think about aspects of our geographical world.

VIEWS OF THE WORLD

Stanley, from the north-east of England, aged 4

Researcher	We're going to look at pictures of a special place – what can we see?
Stanley	Trees and water.
Researcher	Good boy. What do we call a place where there's lots and lots of trees?
Stanley	A rain forest.
Researcher	How do you know that?
Stanley	Because my mummy tells me.
Researcher	Your mummy tells you. Good. Yes, that's a rain forest. A tropical rain forest in a country a long way away. So, Stanley, what do you know about rain forests?
Stanley	It's got snakes and jaguars and . . . I've been to a rain forest.
Researcher	You've been to a rain forest?
Stanley	Yes. I've seen snakes and rattlesnakes and nice green trees.
Researcher	Where did you go to a rain forest?
Stanley	In Spain.
Researcher	In Spain. Your mummy's told you about them. So you know about some of the animals in the forest?
Stanley	Yes.
Researcher	Have you seen rain forests in books?
Stanley	Yes. I've got a rain forest book.

Researcher	Have you?
Stanley	Yes, and it's got a woodpecker in.
Researcher	A woodpecker. Well, let's look at some of the animals who live in a rain forest. Let's see if you know these rain forest animals. What do we have here?
Stanley	Gorilla, and jaguar. Don't know.
Researcher	Very good. This one's called a cheetah.
Stanley	Cheetah.
Researcher	And that one's called an orang-utan. And that one's called a chimpanzee. Do you think people live in rain forests?
Stanley	Some people live in rain forests who's in charge of it.
Researcher	Sometimes people come and cut down the trees. Is that a good idea or a bad idea?
Stanley	A bad idea.
Researcher	Right, Stanley, it's a bad idea. Why shouldn't we cut rain forests down?
Stanley	Because we won't be able to see the flowers, because the trees will fall on top of the flowers.
Researcher	Why else is it wrong to cut down all the trees in the forest?
Stanley	Because we won't see the flowers any more. The flowers get pulled off the branches, and then they go a different colour if you leave them on the park, on the grass.
Researcher	So we should look after rain forests, shouldn't we?
Stanley	Yes.
Researcher	Forests are important in the world. Do you know why forests are so important?
Stanley	Because there's nice things in there and good things. . . .
Researcher	Let's look at one more place. This isn't a rain forest – what do we have here?
Stanley	North Pole, that is.
Researcher	North Pole! Very good. What's this?
Stanley	Ice.
Researcher	Ice and snow. If the weather at the North Pole got hot, what would happen to all the snow at the North Pole?
Stanley	It would just melt.
Researcher	Well done. Do you know where the snow would go to? What would happen to it?
Stanley	It would just go and be gone for ever.
Researcher	Do you know where it would go? Would it just disappear?
Stanley	Yes. . . .
Researcher	Good boy. So we've got some beautiful places in our world, rain forests and the North Pole, and beautiful places with flowers. And we have to take care of them, don't we?

Stanley	Yes.
Researcher	Sometimes people spoil the world by throwing rubbish all over it.
Stanley	Yes, throwing rubbish all over the flowers and all on the floor to make it dirty.
Researcher	Is that wrong?
Stanley	Uh-huh.
Researcher	What should we do with the rubbish?
Stanley	Just throw it in the bin.
Researcher	Do you know where rubbish goes when it's in the bin?
Stanley	The bin men put it in their big truck.
Researcher	They do, and the truck takes it away. Do you know where the truck takes it?
Stanley	To their place.
Researcher	And do you know what happens to it? Can you guess?
Stanley	They put it into a black bin, and then give it to another bin man.
Researcher	Is that what happens to all our rubbish? It gets put into bins?
Stanley	Uh-huh.
Researcher	And the bin men put it into other bins?
Stanley	Uh-huh. . . .
Researcher	Can you think of any other ways we can take care of our beautiful world?
Stanley	From not cutting down the trees.
Researcher	Not cutting down the trees, that's right.
Stanley	Not spoiling the flowers, not treading on the flowers, not going on to the grass and treading all on the flowers.
Researcher	That's right. Why should we look after our world?
Stanley	Yes, it's a very beautiful world.
Researcher	Do you take care of our world?
Stanley	Yes, I do.
Researcher	How could we help other people to know that they must take care of the world?
Stanley	But bad people kill elephants because of their tusks.
Researcher	Right. So do you think zoos are a good idea?
Stanley	Yes.
Researcher	So . . . do you think we should ever kill animals?
Stanley	No, we should look after them.
Researcher	Because they're part of our world, aren't they?
Stanley	But bull fights aren't very nice, are they?
Researcher	No.
Stanley	Yes, because they try and kill all the bulls, don't they?
Researcher	That's right.

Stanley	They tease them.
Researcher	That's right. And we shouldn't tease animals, should we?
Stanley	No, because that's naughty, isn't it?
Researcher	Do you think that when you grow up you will always want to take care of the world?
Stanley	Yes. When I grow up, I'm going to be an animal doctor.
Researcher	Right. That's a very good thing to want to be. So you're going to work very hard at school?
Stanley	Yes. I have to go to London to learn about it.
Researcher	Do you?
Stanley	Uh-huh.
Researcher	Right. So when you grow up, you're going to go to London. . . .
Stanley	Uh-huh.
Researcher	. . . and learn more about animals, because you want to learn how to look after them.
Stanley	Yes.

Daniel, from the USA, aged 4

Researcher	So . . . do you have any idea where those places may be?
Daniel	I think that's Hawaii.
Researcher	It's like Hawaii, isn't it? Good boy, Daniel. What can you see on the picture?
Daniel	Trees and bushes . . .
Researcher	Well done.
Daniel	And a river.
Researcher	Lots of trees. This is a place called a forest. It's called a tropical rain forest.
Daniel	That's . . . is that a tropical rain forest?
Researcher	Yes – do you know about them?
Daniel	'Cos I've seen Ronald McDonald, and he's in a tropical rain forest.
Researcher	Who's been in a tropical rain forest?
Daniel	Ronald McDonald.
Researcher	Who's that?
Daniel	He's a guy . . . and it's a place where you can go and get happy meals. . .
Researcher	Right. So you've seen pictures of a tropical rain forest there. In McDonald's?
Daniel	Yes.
Researcher	Good boy. So . . . do you know what it's like in the forest, Daniel?
Daniel	Uh-huh. Sometimes you can see tigers.

Researcher	Good boy. What else might you see there?
Daniel	And lions . . . and, and . . . and frogs that are coloured. And . . . toucan.
Researcher	Great.
Daniel	Tree frogs.
Researcher	You're an expert.
Daniel	Fox.
Researcher	Have you seen all these things in pictures in McDonald's?
Daniel	Yes.
Researcher	That's wonderful. Well, I have one or two pictures of things which live in the forest.
Daniel	That's, um. . . that's an orang-utan.
Researcher	Well done!
Daniel	That . . . those are chimpanzees.
Researcher	Daniel, you're an expert.
Daniel	That is um . . . a . . . called a cheetah.
Researcher	Daniel, I have talked to a lot of boys and girls, and you're the first one who could tell me the names of all those animals. How do you know so much?
Daniel	Because . . . um . . . I know a lot about animals.
Researcher	Right. How do you know a lot about animals?
Daniel	'Cos, um . . . I've seen them a lot of times.
Researcher	You mean real animals, or you've seen them in books?
Daniel	I've seen them in books, and in zoos.
Researcher	Now, did you know that rain forests have got problems? What kind of problems do rain forests have?
Daniel	Well, sometimes you can get in your car in . . . a lion, an' a tiger or a bear . . .
Researcher	OK. And one of the big problems in rain forests is that people sometimes cut the trees down.
Daniel	Yeah – they shouldn't do that.
Researcher	Good boy. Do you know why they do it?
Daniel	Because they need wood to build their houses.
Researcher	Excellent, Daniel.
Daniel	And firewood for them.
Researcher	And do you know what else they do with the wood they cut down?
Daniel	They make stuff out of it.
Researcher	Right. Why is it a real bad idea to cut the trees down?
Daniel	Because then the rain forest just becomes a whole all dead place.
Researcher	Well done, Daniel. That is right. So what would happen to the animals?
Daniel	They'd die.

Researcher	And the people who live there?
Daniel	They'd die too. . . .
Researcher	And my other place we have . . .
Daniel	Ugh!
Researcher	This place. Now that's not like a rain forest, is it?
Daniel	That is . . . um . . . er . . . that looks like . . . um . . . that looks like . . . um . . . Iceland.
Researcher	Well done. It's a very very snowy land, so that isn't like a rain forest. A rain forest is hot hot, and this is cold cold.
Daniel	I like cool air.
Researcher	Do you? Yes, I do too. If this place got hot like a forest, what would happen to the snow?
Daniel	All of it would melt.
Researcher	What happens to snow when it melts?
Daniel	It becomes . . . everything becomes clean.
Researcher	Right. And where would the snow go?
Daniel	It just evaporates. . . .
Researcher	I can see that you like looking at pictures and reading a lot of books.
Daniel	I read . . . I read stories. And I even have . . . been reading a story about a man named Stuart Liddell. What's the next picture?
Researcher	That's another snowy place.
Daniel	Hey, it has some flowers.
Researcher	Right. So this is such a beautiful world that we live in, and some people don't take care of it. Do you know how people can spoil the world?
Daniel	Like chopping down all the trees and stepping on all the flowers.
Researcher	That's right. Any other ways?
Daniel	Yes. Killing animals . . . killing people.
Researcher	That's good, Daniel. Those are wrong things to do. Another way people can spoil the world is by throwing trash and garbage around the place. That's not a good idea, is it?
Daniel	They should either throw it away or recycle it.
Researcher	Excellent! And do you recycle yours?
Daniel	Sometimes. And we . . . and we throw it away, and give it to the garbage van.
Researcher	Right. So . . . could you just tell me about recycling, 'cos you're an expert on all these things. What does recycling mean?
Daniel	Recycling means saving the trash, and make old things into new things.

Researcher	That's wonderful. What sort of things can we make into new things?
Daniel	Cans.
Researcher	Right.
Daniel	. . . bottles . . . newspaper . . . comics.
Researcher	Right, right. And do you know why we need to make new things out of. . .
Daniel	Old things.
Researcher	. . . waste things.
Daniel	'Cos that helps the world be healthy.
Researcher	That's a wonderful answer, Daniel. It does help the world be healthy. Could you just say a little bit more about that? How does recycling help the world be healthy?
Daniel	By keeping all the trackways in the world clean. And by saving trees and animals.
Researcher	Right. Right. Because if we recycle paper, we're saving . . .
Daniel	Or throw it away, and . . . and . . . and do it to the garbage trucks. . . .
Researcher	Right. Some people think the weather in our world is getting warmer, did you know that? Have you heard about that?
Daniel	And some people think it's getting colder.
Researcher	Right. I wonder which it's doing. So you know we need to take care of trees, 'cos trees are very very important things in our world.
Daniel	Yeah, like the cheetah, the orang-utans and even chimpanzees.
Researcher	Right. And even the people. Why are trees important for people?
Daniel	'Cos they make tree house for kids, or they can use it to be a shady place to rest.
Researcher	Right. That's right.

Stanley and Daniel know a great deal about the world in which they are growing up. They know that forests contain trees, animals and birds. They can identify a number of species. They appreciate that places can be hot or cold, and that if snow gets warmer it melts away or evaporates. They also appreciate that the correct place for waste materials is in rubbish bins. Daniel is even capable of explaining the concept of recycling.

There are, of course, obvious gaps and errors in the knowledge of Stanley and Daniel. This subject will be returned to later in the chapter.

But before pursuing this intriguing topic of knowledge expressed by 4 year olds themselves, attention first focuses on rather more theoretical perspectives on the young child in the geographical world.

As attention turns to this theoretical background, perhaps it should be emphasised that the 'essence' of geography in the early years is concerned with children's developing understanding and appreciation of the human and physical dimensions of the world in which they are growing up. Early years geographical education must therefore take account of wide-ranging theoretical perspectives relating to developing conceptions of the physical environment and understanding of the world, which combine to influence children's thinking and learning in this curriculum area. In short, early years geography is fundamentally about the development of the concepts of 'space' and 'place' and, as we shall see later in this book, a wide range of classroom tasks and related learning activities can contribute to effective learning of these concepts. Practical tasks with which children may engage to promote meaningful learning in geography draw upon a complex theoretical framework. Present space clearly does not allow for a comprehensive overview and analysis of this. Thus it is intended to highlight a number of key elements of the framework and to illuminate these with recent and relevant research evidence.

CONCEPTION OF THE PHYSICAL ENVIRONMENT

Surprisingly little has been written for early years teachers about the origins of children's subject knowledge and conceptual development in the areas of geography and environmental education; that is, areas concerned with cognition of physical systems, spatial relationships, processes and environmental issues. Existing research literature defines and describes the term 'environmental cognition', or the ability to imagine and think about the spatial world, encompassing general ways of thinking about, recognising and organising the physical layout of an environment.

The most substantial body of research on children's conception of the physical environment has been undertaken by Jean Piaget (1960a, 1960b, 1954). His general findings were replicated with much larger samples by Laurendeau and Pinard (1962). Piaget's initial research consideration relating to a child's conception of the world is 'realism', that is, whether external reality is as external and objective for a child as it is for adults. In other words, can a child distinguish the self from the external world? Realism equates to ignoring the existence of self; to drawing boundaries between one's internal world and the physical world. Piaget (1954) describes three processes involved in the evolution of the construction of reality between the ages of 3 and 11. The first of these is the progressive differentiation of the self from physical surroundings, so that an individual can distinguish what comes from within oneself and what is part of the external world. Complete objectivity can never be attained; 'adherences' or parts of internal experience will always remain as part of our conceptions of the physical environment. Five types of adherence exist and overlap: *participation* which is the idea very young children have that objects and processes in the world are linked to our own lives and actions (e.g. the sun follows us as we walk along); *animism*, the belief that physical entities (e.g. clouds) have consciousness; *artificialism*, the tendency of someone to think that everything is made by and for people; *finalism*, the idea of finality without the origins or consequences of an event or process being noticed (e.g. a child says a river flows so as to go into a lake); and *force*, the notion that things 'work' through some kind of energy similar to human muscular force. Alongside these five adherences is the process which Piaget terms phenomenistic causality or phenomenism. For the young child, 'anything can produce anything'. As long as the two facts or objects appear together in observation, they can be interpreted as having a causal relationship. Gradually this idea weakens in the process of growing objectivity and differentiation of self from the physical environment.

The second process involved in the evolution of the construction of reality is 'greater reciprocity' or recognising other points of view. In the early years, children take their immediate perceptions to be true instead of recognising the uniqueness of their own perspective. Piaget uses the example of the young child who thinks that the sun and moon are small globes following us as we walk along; the question does not arise as to whether these globes also follow other people.

Piaget's third process is 'from realism to relativity'. Young children think of everything as absolute substance and quality. Gradually, they come to see objects and phenomena as dependent on each other and relative to us. Once again, the clouds provide an example: at first, these are thought to move by themselves. Gradually, children become aware that they move with the wind, but still believe that they have their own energy and direct themselves. Later, they come to realise that there are other forces which determine the motion of natural objects (e.g. the wind) and that in turn these are dependent upon other external forces. Ultimately, the idea of the existence of a universe of relationships is established. Parallel to this growing relativity of children's understanding of physical properties, objects and qualities is the developing conception that their own ideas are relative to themselves and to their own evaluations of things.

These three processes involved in the young child's construction of reality are summarised in Table 1.1 below. Piaget's account of children's developing understanding of physical causality (Piaget 1960b) follows a similar pattern to his account of developing conception of reality. In both these processes, the young begin by recognising only their personal point of view, thus confusing themselves and the external environment. Gradually, they move towards greater objectivity, reciprocity and relativity.

The essence of Piaget's developmental theory has been challenged and criticised in more recent years, notably by the Soviet development psychologist Vygotsky, who claims that the developmental uniformities found by Piaget are not laws of nature but are 'historically and socially determined'

Table 1.1   A child's construction of reality (from Piaget 1954, 1960a, 1960b)

REALISM	Progressive differentiation of self and environment	GREATER OBJECTIVITY
Self and environment are not distinguished	———————————————	Aware of both an objective and subjective universe
	Decay of 'adherence' (i.e. that physical things are all made by man, are conscious, have force and obey us)	
REALISM	From realism of perception to interpretation	GREATER RECIPROCITY
Own point of view is absolute; reality is what is given immediately	———————————————	Recognises other points of view; reality is what is common to all points of view
	Child regards own perceptions/ dreams as true. Also logical realism, i.e. ideas are subject to the law of the moment and only gradually become relative	
REALISM	Substances and their qualities become more and more dependent upon each other and relative to us	GREATER RELATIVITY
Conceives only of absolute substances and qualities	———————————————	Conceives of a universe of relations
	A growing relativity of ideas in relation to the self and one's evaluation	

Source: Hart and Chawla (1981)

(Vygotsky 1979). His extensive work reveals that cognitive development is influenced by the materials which children experience and the cultural situations in which they are interpreted. While recent research calls Piaget's stages of development into question, the misinterpretations of reality first described by Piaget have been repeatedly found, a fact relevant to the development of programmes of work for teaching and learning experiences in geography and environmental education. Children have a definite tendency to accept the world around them as it is perceived or 'given' through observation. Their own feelings and abilities are also projected into an interpretation of physical entities and space. Thus confusions are created which may lead to erroneous understandings about objects and places. A teacher's role clearly involves having some understanding of such confusions and misinterpretations, and the ability to design learning tasks which take account of them.

UNDERSTANDING THE WORLD

Planning a curriculum and learning experiences about the geographical world need to take account of the learners' understanding of their environment, their interactions with it and sources of information about it. The chief source of environmental knowledge is a child's own direct experience of people, objects and places, supplemented by indirect information such as that from photographs, maps, other people's descriptions and media images. From this combination of sources the child can build up a knowledge of where places and objects are in the world, and a set of ideas and attitudes about such places. In general, the ability to imagine and think about the world around us is referred to as environmental cognition. Environmental knowledge that an individual has already acquired is often described as a 'cognitive map', or mental model of the environment. Such maps or models are personal representations of the world, and their form is complex and controversial. Perhaps the word 'map' is misleading – cognitive maps are not the same as cartographic maps either in physical form or in content. They are sketchy, incomplete, distorted, simplified and idiosyncratic (Devlin 1976, Evans 1980). It is possible to think of them as composed of three elements: places, the spatial relations between places and travel plans (Garling *et al.* 1984). Places refer to the basic spatial units that we attach information to, such as name, function and perceptual characteristics. A place may be a room, building, neighbourhood, town, nation or the whole world. Spatial characteristics of cognitive maps include the distance and direction between places and the inclusion of one place within another (a room is inside a particular building, in a town, in a nation and so on). The concept of travel plans refers to the crucial bridge between the mental world of cognitive maps and practical behaviours (such as finding our way from one place to another) which they support. As would be anticipated, research studies have shown that the more familiar an individual is with an environment, the more accurate and detailed his or her cognitive map will be (Appleyard 1970, Garling *et al.* 1982). The quantity of information stored in memory about a place increases with experience of that place. Inevitably, children have far less direct contact with places than adults, and many environments of the world will be outside their personal experience. Furthermore, differences between children's and adults' cognitive maps reflect not merely differing levels of experience but also different approaches to problem-solving. Again, the research findings of Piaget and his associates are highly relevant to any discussion on the acquisition of cognitive maps. The research of Piaget and Inhelder (1967) probably provides the most influential theory of cognitive development as applied to spatial cognition. This incorporates a study wherein children were asked to sit on a chair and look at a table on which were placed three model mountains. Three other chairs were placed around the table, and a doll was seated on one of them.

From a set of drawings each child was asked to select a view of the scene as the doll would see it. Children below the ages of 7 or 8 typically described the scene as they saw it rather than from the perspective of the doll. Piaget termed this phenomenon egocentrism. During this developmental phase of egocentricity, the child's frame of reference is him/herself. The environment is fragmented and features of it are disconnected. At a later stage, a child's cognitive map is orientated around fixed places in the environment that the child has experience of, but not necessarily the place in which he or she is now situated. Finally, the child's frame of reference assumes more objective representation with accurate spatial connections. Hart and Moore (1973) propose an elaboration of Piaget's findings and suggest that, when developing cognitive mapping abilities, children progress through three sequential stages involving progressively more complex frames of reference. First, there is an undifferentiated 'egocentric reference system' in which the image consists only of those elements in the environment that are of great personal significance. Second, there is a 'partially co-ordinated reference system' in which several clusters of points demonstrate a knowledge of the relationships between landmarks (e.g. distinctive features such as buildings, monuments) and paths (e.g. streets, footpaths, rivers), but where these clusters are not related to each other. Finally, children develop an 'operationally co-ordinated and hierarchically integrated reference system' in which the environmental image is organised into a single spatial reference system.

Subsequent studies have generally confirmed Piaget's observations that pre-school children demonstrate egocentrism, though there is debate and controversy on whether this is a reflection of a truly different way of thinking or a slow increase in the quantity of environmental information and cognitive skills (Bell *et al.* 1990). Research done in large-scale environments has found young children to be more capable of accurate cognitive mapping than that done in studies using models (Cousins *et al.* 1983). Further work on the accuracy and complexity of cognitive maps (Siegel and White 1975) suggests that there are four sequential developmental stages in children's representations of the spatial environment. First, landmarks (distinctive features which are important to the child) are noticed and remembered, followed by paths between landmarks. At stage three, landmarks and paths are organised into clusters or minimaps, and, finally, these clusters along with other features are correctly co-ordinated into an overall framework or complete representation of the environment. Thus Siegel and White's evidence, which draws on a number of different empirical studies, supports the existence of a series of developmental stages in cognitive mapping ability. Despite widespread support for this theory, it should be noted that related evidence derives in the main from indirect methods of testing children's memories and knowledge of their environment, such as maps and models. Other studies, which have directly tested environmental cognition (e.g. Cornell and Heth 1983) by taking children on walks outdoors, have revealed the ease with which young subjects can accurately retrace a route, having only walked along it once before. Darvizeh and Spencer (1984) show that children's memory for a route can be significantly improved when their attention is drawn to appropriate landmarks along the way. Thus they conclude that, instead of explaining children's developing environmental cognition by a series of fixed stages, it may be more appropriate to consider their achievement in terms of their ability to apply efficient strategies for selecting appropriate information from the environment. Even very young children can remember a great deal about a route after limited experience of it, but they may not be as aware of or knowledgeable about the route as older subjects because of their more limited ability to note information about it as they travel along. A detailed review and discussion of research on the development of spatial knowledge and a child's changing environmental needs is provided by Spencer et al. (1989). They emphasise the processes of environmental cognition (cognitive mapping, acquisition of spatial information, images of places) as well as its development. Further reference to each of these processes will be made in the context of discussion of practical examples, throughout the remaining chapters of this volume.

NEAR AND FAR

The development of environmental cognition covers a range of space-related concepts, including the child's developing body-image, the location of objects in close space and understanding of geographical scale space, and the emergence of concepts about distant places. Examples in this book cover this range and illuminate the young child's ever-expanding awareness of the physical world. Some researchers (Welsh and Blasch 1980) have stressed the importance of a developmental sequence of spatial understanding, wherein the child must first achieve an 'integrated image' of body-layout with body-part co-ordination, extend this framework of reference to the immediate world, with a focus on location of objects in near space, and then proceed outward from this to consider and understand the spatial inter-relationships between objects and places. Others (Pick and Lockman 1981) argue that an individual does not have to achieve complete mastery of the first frame of reference before proceeding to the next. Furthermore, once mastered, we can use any one or a combination of these reference systems. Spencer et al. (1989) provide a detailed review of each stage/frame of reference with discussion of further research evidence that illuminates this developmental question.

One of the most important messages that emerges from research done in this general field of environmental cognition and development of spatial awareness is that young children are remarkably good at learning. They are certainly ready for and are indeed using geographical concepts and understandings as early as 4–5 years of age. They have thought about their immediate space and local environment: about routes and landmarks, about distant places, about our planet, and have acquired skills of investigation and understanding. The following brief glimpse at research evidence certainly reveals a strong basis for the foundation of geographical understanding in the early years.

Cornell and Hay (1984) show the success of personal experience or active exploration in route learning. Children aged 5–8 were asked to view a route either by a slide presentation, a video-tape or by walking the route with a leader. The route was viewed only once, then they had to retrace it in the same medium. Results showed little difference between children using slide or video-tape, but significantly fewer errors were made by the children who actively experienced the route. Landmarks and directions were recalled, and subjects could find their way back to the start.

Muir and Blaut (1969) demonstrate the ability of young children to learn about mapping from aerial photographs. They used photographs to teach a group of 5–6 year olds about maps, then compared these children to others who were taught without photographs. The 'experimental' group performed very much better in map tests than the non-photograph group. Also in the realm of early years mapwork, Atkins (1981) taught children aged 4–5 about maps, globes and compass directions, then compared this group to another which had not received instruction. The experimental group performed better than the control group in tests immediately after the instruction and again a year later. Both the Muir and Blaut and Atkins studies demonstrate abilities in the field of 'graphicacy' in children much younger than the age that many have associated with the commencement of mapwork understanding. Blades and Spencer (1986) report similar findings and conclude that children may well be able to learn skills of mapwork before they reach the 'projective' stage of spatial development (discussed at greater length in Chapter 4) at the age of 7–8. Following on from this early study, Blades and Spencer (1987a) carried out an experiment to test children's understanding of maps and their ability to cope with symbols. Four to six year olds were asked to name features on a specially designed map.

Although imaginary, the map was intended to represent a possible urban environment, with roads (grey) lined by small and large houses (red). There were two roundabouts at road junctions. To the south-west two roads crossed by bridges over a river (blue) and to the east there was a road bridge over a railway line (black). In the north-east, a large irregular area was coloured green to represent a park or playing field. The map also included symbols for particular buildings; two 'churches' (shown as black crosses), two 'schools' (shown in 'playgrounds') and in the south-east corner, three black oblongs to represent a 'station' next to the railway lines.

(Blades and Spencer 1987a)

One hundred and eight children between the ages of 4 and 6 took part in this experiment. Half were asked to name the symbols as each one was pointed out to them on the map. There were ten symbols altogether (road, river, park, roundabout, bridge, school, church, railway, station and house). The other half of the children were given the names of each feature and were asked to point to an example of the symbol representing that feature on the map. By the age of 6, nearly all the children could identify the majority of the symbols on the map. Even the 4 year olds could recognise at least half of the symbols.

> Very few children failed to recognise anything at all on the map or describe it simply in terms of lines, shapes or colours. It was easier for children to find examples of named features than to have to suggest names for the symbols on the map. Not all the symbols were of equal difficulty; roads, river, and park were easily identified by nearly all the children, but the symbols for station, church and school were harder to identify, though by the age of 6, children were able to suggest quite appropriate definitions (such as 'hospital' or 'factory').
> The results from this experiment and the findings from the research into children's ability to understand aerial photographs indicate that young children can appreciate a view of the world from above, even when, as in the case with the map, the view is one that is conventionalised and includes symbols.
>
> (Spencer *et al.* 1989)

A further element of mapwork that has come under research scrutiny is co-ordinates. Many maps use co-ordinate reference systems so that particular locations can be identified by a grid reference relating to a series of horizontal and vertical grid lines. While some research (Piaget *et al.* 1960) has suggested that children cannot accurately locate a point in space until around the age of 8, other findings reinforce the view that much younger children are capable of demonstrating skills of graphicacy. Somerville and Bryant (1985) show that 4–6 year olds are capable of using co-ordinates in simple tasks. In their studies, children were shown an opaque square board that was placed over two rods; one rod protruded from the left or right side of the board, thus providing a horizontal co-ordinate, and the other protruded from the top or bottom of the board, providing a vertical co-ordinate. The subjects were asked to extrapolate from the visible portions of the rods and indicate where they thought the rods crossed under the board by selecting one of four given points marked on top of the board. Results showed that children as young as 4½ years could do this task successfully, and that most aged 6½ could be successful in a number of variations on the basic task. Further experiments by Blades and Spencer (1987a) investigate whether young children can use a grid reference system. Four to six year olds were tested using a board that incorporated 16 sunken squares in a 4 × 4 layout. Each square contained a different picture, hidden by a cardboard cover. Vertical and horizontal co-ordinate lines were drawn across the board and intersected over the centre of each covered picture. The vertical co-ordinates were numbered 1, 2, 3, 4, and the horizontal co-ordinates were lettered a, b, c, d. The children were given a grid reference card (e.g. 4a, 1c) and a copy of the correct hidden picture was fixed to the back of the card. The children's task was to find the appropriate square on the board for a given grid reference. After a square had been selected, the cover could be removed so that its picture could be checked for match with that on the back of the grid reference card. Results showed that the majority of the 6 year olds could perform this task successfully; but only a small percentage of the younger children could do so.

A follow-up experiment was performed with another group of children of similar age. This time each grid co-ordinate was labelled with a different colour. (It was hypothesised that perhaps in the original experiment the younger children may have been confused because they were not proficient with the alphabet or numbers.) The grid reference in this second experiment was a card with two colours on it, one for the horizontal co-ordinate and one for the vertical co-ordinate. Results this time showed that half the 4 year olds and the majority of 5 and 6 year olds were successful in the given task, confirming the hypothesis that results in the previous experiment may have been affected by inability to read letters or numbers. The combined results of Somerville and Bryant and Blades and Spencer suggest that 4 year olds are capable of using a grid co-ordinate reference system. As with other elements of mapwork, we may conclude that young children's competence in this area has for a long time been underestimated and underdeveloped in school-based learning tasks.

A similar trend emerges in the area of map use. Bluestein and Acredolo (1979) showed children aged 3 to 5 a map of a small rectangular room with table, chairs and four identical green boxes which could serve as hiding places for a small toy. The boxes were placed at the mid-point of each wall. In one corner of the room was a door and in each of the other three corners were objects, e.g. a red box. The children were shown on a map the box that contained the hidden toy. Then they were asked to find the correct box in the actual room. The children were shown the map either inside or outside the room and it was either correctly orientated with the room or rotated through 180 degrees relative to it. Of the children who saw the map in the room correctly orientated, half the 3 year olds, three-quarters of the 4 year olds and all the 5 year olds could find the toy successfully. Only the 5 year olds could use the map correctly when it was rotated. A key conclusion from this work is that children as young as 3 years can use a map in certain circumstances.

Other experiments confirm that children of a very young age can use a map to find a particular object or place. In so doing, they show a tendency to refer to landmarks on the map or on the 'ground'. The ability to use landmarks effectively has been demonstrated by indoor 'laboratory' experiments (Acredolo *et al.* 1975) as well as by studies of children finding their way in actual environments (Darvizeh and Spencer 1984). Blades and Spencer (1986) also suggest that it is possible to teach 4 year olds how to orientate simple maps. They showed children how to align an incorrectly orientated map so that it corresponded to a layout before they attempted to use the map to find a place in the layout. The majority of the children who were shown how to align the map learnt to do this speedily and could apply the same skills in different situations. A more complex test has been devised (Blades and Spencer 1987b) to find out if young children can use a map to navigate through an environment that is not completely visible. A 25-metre-long maze was drawn on the surface of a school playground. Within this maze were three T-junctions, and large screens were placed across the pathways in front of the junctions in order to limit the children's view across the maze. Wooden boxes were placed across the paths to serve as 'roadblocks' and the position of these was hidden by the screens. Thus the children could not see them before making a route choice at each of the T-junctions. The subjects were then given a map of the maze showing the positions of the roadblocks. This map was attached to a clipboard so that it could be carried as they walked through the maze. Their task was to navigate through the maze without bumping into any of the roadblocks. Sixty children in five age groups between 3 to 6 years had six trials each at the maze. For each trial, the positions of the roadblocks were changed. The majority of children in all age groups except the very youngest were able to use their maps effectively to find their route through the maze.

A few children were generally successful, but made errors in particular trials. Some children were observed pointing along the route with their finger on the map as they walked through the maze, and there were occasions when they failed to update their position on the map. For example, a child approaching the third T-junction in the maze might be seen pointing at the second T-junction on the map, and this sometimes resulted in an incorrect turn at the third junction. All three junctions in the maze were identical and this may have sometimes confused the children. To see if this was a problem we repeated the same experiment with a further 60 children of the same age, but placed distinctive landmarks at each junction (these were different brightly coloured objects). These landmarks were marked on the map with appropriate colours. In this condition the overall performance of the children improved, which suggested that the children were able to take advantage of the presence of the landmarks to help them find their way through the maze. The maze experiment demonstrated that from the age of 4 years children could use a simple map to follow a route, and their improved performance when the landmarks were present suggests that the children were sensitive to any additional information provided by the map.

(Spencer *et al.* 1989)

Thus a number of studies demonstrate that very young children can use simple maps to find places, to follow routes and to locate landmarks.

Untrained children from the age of 3 or 4 years have an appreciation of a two-dimensional representation of a given area. This is considerably earlier than might be expected from the interpretations of Piaget's theory of spatial development, which imply that such young children are too limited in their understanding of spatial relationships.

(Spencer *et al.* 1989)

The concluding message for educators is, of course, that it is feasible to start teaching elements of mapwork and aspects of the use of maps to children as young as 4 years of age.

Further illumination of young children's capacity for geographical/environmental learning is provided by research on their images and understanding of distant places, of which they have no direct experience. Once again, a similar pattern of conclusions emerges: children are remarkably good at learning about other lands and peoples, albeit from secondary source materials. They have a 'world inside their heads', derived from constant interactions with the media (TV, films, newspapers), travel advertisements, books and descriptions by other people. Young children know that there is a 'world out there' – from the news, from international take-away food shops, from foreign presenters of children's TV programmes and from story books, among numerous other incidental contacts with distant places and people of other nationalities. This topic will be explored at greater depth in Chapter 4, but at this stage further dimensions of young children's geographical learning must be introduced.

Considerable evidence has already been referred to which demonstrates that children are efficient learners and bring a sound basis of geographical knowledge into the classroom as and when they start school. Yet they also bring gaps in knowledge, erroneous knowledge and perhaps biased/ stereotypical knowledge which the teacher needs to be well aware of in order to design appropriate learning tasks. Research on children's images of distant lands illustrates this point well.

Piaget made a substantial contribution to the understanding of a child's developing concepts of his or her own area, town, region and country, paying attention to conceptual development rather than sources of information. According to Piaget's study (1960a) there are three broad stages in the child's development of the idea of country. In the first instance, a country is 'simply a unit along with towns and districts', which the child believes are of similar size. Next is a stage in which the child knows that a district is within a country and yet it is spoken of as if it were a piece of land 'enclosed within a foreign country'. In the third stage, the child acquires a correct idea of the relationship – one can belong to a town, a district and a country at the same time. This work does not consider yet more distant places. Later studies have replicated and extended Piaget's work. Piché (1981) interviewed 5–8 year olds on their expanding understanding of the world, from most local to most distant places. It was found that 5 year olds will describe a building, a district, a city and a country as the same kind of place because one can go there. For many children of this age, all places that are not home are in a category of 'elsewhere'. This fact aside, a great deal of information is acquired by young minds about 'elsewhere' from the media and other incidental contacts. The question must then be asked – what is the status of this 'knowledge' that is acquired? Tajfel (1981) argues that children are capable of absorbing attitudes and prejudices about other people and nations well before they have any factual information about them:

> The young child is at an early, but important stage in the development of a social identity – related to the in-and-out groups as specified by the surrounding culture; and the acquisition and interpretation of factual information about own group and other groups will be related to this frame of reference. In other words, information will be selectively sought, received and remembered, in ways that are supportive of pre-existing (pre-judged) categories.
>
> (Tajfel 1981)

Stillwell and Spencer (1974) demonstrated the role of educational media in changing children's knowledge of and feelings for other countries. They investigated the influence of wallcharts and classroom displays on the development of primary school pupils' attitudes towards other nations. Nine year olds were interviewed about their knowledge of and feelings towards four countries: India, Germany, the USA and the USSR. Displays of wallcharts depicting street scenes, transport, local dress and the world position of those countries were then put up in the classroom for a week, with no accompanying teaching or discussion. After this time, the children were interviewed once again, and revealed a significant increase in information about all four countries. Of noticeable importance was the children's changing preferences for these countries. In the initial interviews they had been strongly pro-USA and anti-German, with India and the USSR being on the positive side of neutral. After the displays and increased knowledge about these places, the USA remained popular, Germany became strongly positive, the USSR remained relatively neutral, and India moved to a position of negative preference. Children initially stressed the differences between Britain and Germany, claiming that towns, clothes and skin colour were 'different from here'. The USA was strongly supported initially as it was believed to be 'like us, only better'. These findings are in line with those of Jaspars *et al*. (1963) who found that children preferred the countries that they saw as near to their own in cognitive space. In the Stillwell and Spencer experiment, initially the USSR and India had been largely unknown lands – neither apparently like us nor obviously different. The effect of the displays was remarkable – children who had previously perceived great differences between Britain and Germany saw photographs of similar environments. Thus preferences were shifted from the negative to the positive. The USA was confirmed as 'bigger and better', and the USSR was confirmed as being just a little different from Britain. India shifted its position to being negative, through pictures that set a scene of being 'not like us'. From this study, it may be concluded that the provision of accurate information in educational circumstances may not necessarily increase understanding and resultant positive acceptance of a nation and its people. This study was conducted with 9 year olds, but its results are transferable to a younger age. Stereotypes exist in young minds, and knowledge and information may be used to measure the similarity of a nation against our own, which is inevitably valued.

The popular media also provide a strong influence on the development of the 'world inside children's minds'. A survey of American children's images of Africa (Birns in Spencer *et al*. [1989]) reveals words such as 'wild animals, jungles, witch doctors, and Daktari' as being uppermost in their minds – conjured up largely by a popular television programme. Along similar lines, Storm (1984) reported word-association tests with children of primary school age. Results showed that the words most commonly associated with 'Africa' were 'lions', 'heat', 'snakes', 'elephants', 'trees', 'tigers', 'palm trees' and 'black people', conjuring up images of the exotic, colour and perhaps the excitement of Africa derived from 'jungle' films and programmes on TV – images far removed from many of the realities of everyday life there today in the shape of poverty and cities.

Crucial issues to bear in mind when approaching and planning the study of distant lands with young children are thus stereotyping, bias and often incomplete or erroneous subject knowledge which may be brought to the classroom. Perhaps it should also be pointed out that the situation may not be helped by a teacher's genuine ignorance of particular facts or biased viewpoint about a place, perhaps arising from specific media coverage or a holiday in an atypical part of the land. The teacher's task is thus a complex and difficult one. It is to build upon the existing knowledge base of the children, yet the teacher has to bear in mind the problems and limitations of this as identified. In an ideal world, by being provided with appropriate accurate information, leading to an appreciation of environmental conditions different from our own, and by building up a more coherent and complete picture of the place being studied, the confused infant will emerge into an adult with accurate and unbiased views of people and places. Unfortunately, the world of school classrooms is perhaps not that ideal.

KNOWLEDGE OR CONCERN?

So far this chapter has illuminated and discussed aspects of children's early learning about the geographical world. It has, I hope, delivered the powerful message that young children are remarkably good at learning about their surroundings, even though elements of this resultant subject knowledge may be incomplete, biased or prejudiced. Research evidence has traditionally concentrated on what children know and can do: the development of those elements of knowledge, skills and concepts which underpin geographical and environmental understanding. Yet if environmental education is at least in part about the development of awareness and positive attitudes towards taking care of the world, it follows that an equally important area for consideration in the planning of appropriate teaching and learning tasks should be the development of children's attitudes towards and concern *for* the environment. An ongoing research study at the University of Durham (Palmer, 1992a, 1992b, 1993) provides some interesting and important insights into the development of both subject knowledge and concern. This research study as a whole investigates 'emergent environmentalism', that is, the development of subject knowledge and concern for the environment in both children and adults. Formative influences and significant life experiences of environmentally aware adults are discussed elsewhere (Palmer 1992a) but, in this context, the element of the study involving pre-school children is worthy of detailed description and discussion, as it illuminates many issues relevant to geographical and environmental education in the early years that will be elaborated upon at later stages in this volume.

One hundred and twenty children aged between 4.0 and 5.1 years were involved in the first phase of the research into early childhood learning. Sixty live in the towns of Palo Alto and Los Altos in the southern San Francisco Bay area of California, USA and 60 are from schools in Co. Durham in the north-east of England. All were attending nursery schools at the time of interview. An autobiographical, discussion approach was used to find out as much as possible about the children's knowledge of and concern for certain environmental issues. Each child was interviewed individually and discussion between researcher and child was stimulated with the aid of photographs, as outlined below. Attention was focused on four well-known issues of concern to the world today, namely the importance of trees and rain forest destruction, endangered species, global warming and waste materials. The aims of the interviews were to ascertain:

- what the children knew and understood about these issues, if anything;
- the sources of their knowledge;
- the extent to which the children were aware of these topics as issues about which people should be concerned.

Conversation with each child was initiated by showing pictures of trees in a tropical rain forest. The subject was asked to talk about what he or she could see and what he or she thought the place shown in the picture would be like. Immediately it became apparent whether the child was familiar with words such as 'trees', 'forest' and 'tropical rain forest'. The questions 'Who/What do you think lives there?' and 'Where would you have to go to find places like this?' led to insights into the children's knowledge or lack of knowledge about animals, birds, plants and people of the forests as well as their location in the world. After being given the opportunity for spontaneous reference to forest life, the children were shown pictures of a number of creatures of the forest (orang-utan, chimpanzee, cheetah) to test identification skills and act as a possible lead into discussion about conservation of animals and endangered species. It was then suggested that sometimes the forests change because people cut down the trees. This section of the discussion elicited views on whether this is a good or bad idea, why it is done, and reasons for the importance of trees in our world. The general atmosphere of the rain forest was considered, and children reminded that these are hot, wet places.

By way of contrast, pictures were then shown of the North Pole, and subjects were asked to describe what they could see and to say how this location is different from the rain forests. The key questions at this stage of the interview were about weather conditions, notably about what would happen if the weather changed at the North Pole and it became a much warmer place. Would it still look the same? This enabled the interviewer to find out if the children understood basic scientific ideas relating to global warming, that is, that snow melts if it gets warmer and that melting snow produces water.

Next the interviewer introduced the topic of waste materials by drawing attention to the fact that all the pictures observed are of clean, tidy places in our world, and that sometimes people spoil the landscape by throwing down litter. The children were asked about appropriate places to put waste, and about how their own families deal with discarded materials. Children who demonstrated an understanding of recycling and waste removal were asked further questions about these processes.

Finally, an attempt was made to round off the discussion with thoughts about the importance of keeping our world 'clean' and taking care of it in general; in other words, to try to establish whether the children did have any sense of concern and responsibility for our planet and its life.

It should be noted that one individual conducted all the interviews and used the same photographs, format and 'lead' questions in all of them. Thus reliability was established, as far as was considered possible, in open-ended discussion and qualitative research of this kind.

Extracts from the interviews with Stanley (UK) and Daniel (USA) were provided at the beginning of the chapter. There now follows a series of abbreviated extracts illuminating aspects of other children's thinking on each of the issues discussed.

On rain forests, trees and animals

Carl (UK)

Researcher	Can you tell me what you can see in the picture?
Carl	A river. The trees.
Researcher	Trees. That's right. Lots of trees. Do you know what we call a place where there's lots of trees?
Carl	A forest.
Researcher	Well done. This is a forest called a rain forest or a jungle, in a country a long way away. What do you think it's like in the forest?
Carl	Nice and warm.
Researcher	What would you see in the forest?
Carl	Tigers, lions, elephants.
Researcher	How do you know about forests?
Carl	'Cos it's very hot there. . . . [more discussion about animals]
Researcher	Have you seen pictures of them before? Where have you seen pictures of forests? Have you seen jungles on the television?
Carl	Yes.
Researcher	Do you think people live in the rain forests? Could you tell me about the people – what are they like?
Carl	Soldiers.
Researcher	What do the soldiers do in the forests?
Carl	Eat some food.
Researcher	What do you think they eat?
Carl	Cabbage . . . and carrots . . . and potatoes . . . beefburgers . . . and seafood . . . and chips.
Researcher	Sometimes people cut the trees down. Do you know why they do that?
Carl	Because they grow.
Researcher	Is it a good idea to cut down the trees?

Carl	Yes. If they fall on you, you'll die.
Researcher	So when they cut the trees down, what do they do with them, Carl?
Carl	Make them little.
Researcher	Right. And the trees that they've cut away – what do they do with those? Could they use them?
Carl	Don't know.

John (USA)

Researcher	What do you see there?
John	A lake. . .
Researcher	Right. And . . .?
John	Palm trees.
Researcher	Lots of trees. So do you know what sort of place this is?
John	A desert?
Researcher	Ah, no, not a desert. Deserts don't have too many trees and water. It's called a forest.
John	I wanted to say that.
Researcher	Right, no problem. And this forest is called a tropical rain forest. Not heard of one of those?
John	No.
Researcher	Right. I wonder what lives in a tropical rain forest. I wonder why it's called a rain forest. Could you guess the answer: Why do you think it's called a rain forest?
John	Because there's lots of . . . like, rain.
Researcher	That's right, John. And I wonder who lives in the forest. Can you think?
John	A lion?
Researcher	May do. Right. Good boy. Lots of animals live here.
John	Tiger?
Researcher	Lots and lots of animals, and here's some of them. So what do we see here?
John	A cheetah.
Researcher	Well done! Good boy – how did you know that was a cheetah?
John	Because my brother is older than me . . .
Researcher	And he shows you pictures of them?
John	Yes.
Researcher	Good. And what sort of animals are here that live in the forest?
John	Monkeys.
Researcher	They're monkeys – and these are another sort of monkey, these are chimpanzees. And the forest has frogs and birds and beautiful flowers.

John	At Rhode Island I found lots of frogs . . .
Researcher	You know, John, these forests have got problems because sometimes people chop the trees down. Do you know why they do that?
John	Why?
Researcher	Well, they use the wood.
John	Oh, yeah – to use wood for fire.
Researcher	To make a fire. What else may they use the wood for?
John	Make a house.
Researcher	Right. And do you think it's a good idea to chop the trees down?
John	No.
Researcher	No it isn't. Why is it a bad idea?
John	Because the trees will die and we need them to breathe air.
Researcher	We need them to . . .?
John	To breathe air.
Researcher	How do you know about that?
John	My mom told me.

Nicola (USA)

Researcher	Well, here's my first picture . . .
Nicola	Where did you take it?
Researcher	. . . isn't that a beautiful place? Where do you think that might be?
Nicola	South America?
Researcher	Good girl! It is.
Nicola	I know where trees grow . . . because, you see, I . . . er . . . I know a lot.
Researcher	How do you know so much?
Nicola	My daddy knows a lot and he told me.
Researcher	Your daddy told you.
Nicola	Yep.
Researcher	Right. Now this place is called a rain forest.
Nicola	Why?
Researcher	Why do you think? Could you guess why?
Nicola	Because it rains a lot there.
Researcher	Well done! It rains a lot.
Nicola	I'm smart!
Researcher	. . . and it's hot and steamy . . .
Nicola	I'm very smart, because my daddy is smart, and he taught me how to be smart.
Researcher	Do you know about things that live in the rain forest?
Nicola	No, I just know about the trees and the rain.

Researcher	Good girl. Well, you tell me about the trees. Are they important?
Nicola	Yes, very . . .
Researcher	You're right, Nicky. Why are trees very important?
Nicola	Because they make paper . . . and they can make lots of things . . . you can lie down by it . . . and you can make things, and they're very good for you, and you can pick . . . um . . . um . . . fruits off of them, and you can . . . you can climb on them . . .
Researcher	You're right, Nicky. And lots of animals live in the rain forest . . . here's some pictures.
Nicola	Monkeys. I know that's a baby monkey. And that's . . . a . . . leopard. . . . leopard or a cheetah.
Researcher	It's a cheetah, you're right.
Nicola	I have a leopard toy, it's kind of like this . . . this one. And I even have this little panda, but it's not real. Why are they chopping down the trees?
Researcher	Could you guess why?
Nicola	To make things out of . . . they make paper, and make houses . . .
Researcher	That's right, Nicky. So what do you think may happen if the trees get chopped down?
Nicola	There'll be . . . um . . . let me think . . . a valley or something, and there won't be any trees to um . . . to sit down by.
Researcher	OK. And what would happen to the animals?
Nicola	Um . . . the animals would have . . . the monkeys won't have . . . the monkeys couldn't climb and the cheetahs couldn't climb . . . and the flowers wouldn't grow on the trees . . . um . . . the beautiful leaves wouldn't grow.

Dean (UK)

Researcher	Can you tell me what you can see in the pictures?
Dean	Water . . . and trees.
Researcher	Lots of trees. Do you know what we call a place with lots and lots of trees?
Dean	A forest.
Researcher	That's right. Now this is a big forest or a jungle in a country a long way away from here. So what do you think it's like in the forest?
Dean	Yuk.
Researcher	What's it like?
Dean	Yuk.
Researcher	Yuk. Why is it yuk?

Dean	I don't know.
Researcher	Who lives in the forest, Dean?
Dean	Robin Hood.
Researcher	Do you think animals live here?
Dean	Sheep . . .
Researcher	Anything else?
Dean	. . . and cows.
Researcher	Do you think any people live in the jungle?
Dean	Mowgli.
Researcher	Sometimes people cut down the trees. Why do you think they do that?
Dean	Because they get long.
Researcher	Because they get long. So is it a good idea to cut down trees? What do they do with the trees when they cut them down?
Dean	Take them to the tip.
Researcher	And throw them away? Is that a good thing to do?
Dean	Yep.

Jeffrey (USA)

Researcher	What can you see here?
Jeffrey	Um . . . I can see some water.
Researcher	Right. And what else can you see here?
Jeffrey	Um . . . trees.
Researcher	Lots of trees. So this is a place where we have lots and lots of trees. Do you know what we call a place where there are lots of trees?
Jeffrey	Water?
Researcher	We call this a forest.
Jeffrey	Forest . . .
Researcher	This place is called a tropical rain forest.
Jeffrey	A tropical rain forest.
Researcher	I wonder why it's called a rain forest.
Jeffrey	Because it rains so much.
Researcher	That's very good – because it has lots of rain. It's very hot and it has lots of rain. And . . . I wonder who lives in the forest?
Jeffrey	Ah . . . snakes, foxes . . . and wolves.
Researcher	And wolves.
Jeffrey	Specially in the dark . . . specially when it's night time.
Researcher	How do you know about forests, Jeffrey?
Jeffrey	Because I've seen pictures.
Researcher	You've seen pictures. Pictures in books?
Jeffrey	Yes.

Researcher	Let's look at some pictures of some of the animals who live in the forest.
Jeffrey	A gorilla . . . I think I've seen him when I've been to the zoo.
Researcher	You saw him in the zoo? Right, good boy.
Jeffrey	And I saw these . . . ah . . .
Researcher	They're called cheetahs . . .
Jeffrey	Cheetahs . . . I saw some cheetahs. Do they have any . . . do you have any snakes?
Researcher	There are snakes in the forest . . .
Jeffrey	My dad's seen snakes . . . he's seen snakes . . . when he's been running . . . [more discussion about animals, birds, flowers]
Researcher	Do you know why they might do that? [cut down trees]
Jeffrey	Why? To make a house or a cabin.
Researcher	Right, good boy. So they might use the wood from the trees to make their house. So is that a good idea to cut down trees?
Jeffrey	No. [shakes head]
Researcher	Why is it not a good idea?
Jeffrey	Because then you waste wood.
Researcher	That's very good.

On warming of the world

Carl (UK)

Researcher	What do you think this place is like?
Carl	Snowy.
Researcher	So is it hot or cold?
Carl	Cold.
Researcher	If it got hot, what do you think would happen to the snow?
Carl	Melt.
Researcher	Well done, that's very good. And what happens to snow when it melts?
Carl	It would be gone.
Researcher	Do you know where it would go to?
Carl	To the forest.
Researcher	You think the snow would go to the forest?
Carl	Everywhere.
Researcher	Right. So the snow would go from the North Pole . . . and where would it go to?
Carl	To Santa Claus' house.
Researcher	To Santa Claus' house?
Carl	'Cos Santa Claus makes the snow, doesn't he?

Nicola (USA)

Nicola	Um . . .
Researcher	That's a different place, isn't it?
Nicola	I know . . . Alaska. My daddy has went to Alaska, and I never seen a picture of Alaska, that's why I guessed Alaska.
Researcher	Right. Why did you think it was Alaska?
Nicola	Because it had snow.
Researcher	Good girl. So that's a cold place . . .
Nicola	And I saw the mountains, and decided it was Alaska.
Researcher	Good, Nicky. Now some people think that the world we live in is getting a warmer place.
Nicola	I know that.
Researcher	How do you know that?
Nicola	I know that because it seems like it's getting warmer here . . . and, do you know what, my tangerines are gotten riper now on my tangerine tree and you can eat them.
Researcher	Really? At this time of year, in the winter?
Nicola	Yeah. My plums always . . . um . . . my plum tree always . . . does it, and . . . um . . . I think, in the summer.
Researcher	So if the world gets warmer, Nicky, what might happen to places like Alaska and the North Pole?
Nicola	Um . . . the snow will melt.
Researcher	And where will it go?
Nicola	To . . . um . . .
Researcher	What happens to snow when it melts?
Nicola	Um . . . it'll go . . . to a different place, or somewhere.

Jocelyn (USA)

Researcher	What do you think this place is like?
Jocelyn	Snowy.
Researcher	So is this a hot place?
Jocelyn	No!
Researcher	If this place got hot, what would happen to the snow?
Jocelyn	Melt!
Researcher	Right. You know about that . . .
Jocelyn	I like deep, fresh snow.
Researcher	If the snow melts, do you know where it goes?
Jocelyn	Where?
Researcher	Do you know? What may happen to it?
Jocelyn	Turns into water.
Researcher	Right. And where does the water go?
Jocelyn	Into bays.

Researcher	Well done! Do you know what a bay is?
Jocelyn	Place where a lot of water runs, and where people come to sit on the sand.
Researcher	Right. And then . . . where does the water in the bays go to?
Jocelyn	Well, I don't really know that.
Researcher	Well, that's part of the sea, you know, the big oceans in our world.

Eleanor (USA)

Researcher	. . . What do you think would happen to the snow?
Eleanor	The snow would melt.
Researcher	Well done. Where would it go?
Eleanor	Where?
Researcher	Mmm. Where does snow go when it melts? What happens to it?
Eleanor	It . . . it disappears.
Researcher	Right. Do you know where it disappears to?
Eleanor	The water.
Researcher	Into the water. And where's the water?
Eleanor	It's the sea.
Researcher	That's right. So if that place got warm, there would be no snow.
Eleanor	There'd be water . . . it would all be water.

Stephanie (UK)

Researcher	Let's look at another place. Is this a hot place?
Stephanie	No.
Researcher	What's this?
Stephanie	Snow.
Researcher	Snow. This is a snowy place. And if this snowy place got warmer, what would happen to the snow?
Stephanie	It would melt.
Researcher	Well done. What does that mean?
Stephanie	It means that the snow won't come.
Researcher	The snow won't come. The melted snow wouldn't be there. Do you know where it would go? When snow melts, do you know where it goes to?
Stephanie	Under the ground.

Rachel (USA)

| Researcher | What's the weather like here? |

Rachel	Cold.
Researcher	How do you know it's cold?
Rachel	Because I can see the snow.
Researcher	If it got warm, what would happen to the snow?
Rachel	It would melt.
Researcher	Right. Do you know what that means? Where does the snow go when it melts?
Rachel	Away.
Researcher	Do you know where it goes to?
Rachel	The sky?

On waste materials

Carl (UK)

Carl	Have to put them in the bin.
Researcher	Well done. Why should we not throw it down on the ground?
Carl	'Cos it's naughty.
Researcher	And all this rubbish we put in the bin, do you know what happens to it?
Carl	Thrown away. . . and the bin men.
Researcher	Good. What do the bin men do with it?
Carl	Throw it in the tip.
Researcher	Well done. Can you tell me about the tip? What's the tip like?
Carl	Nasty.
Researcher	Full of rubbish.
Carl	Stinks.
Researcher	Does the rubbish stay in the tip for always?
Carl	All day.
Researcher	Does all our rubbish go to the tip? Is it a good place for it?
Carl	Yes.
Researcher	So the bin man takes all our rubbish and puts it in the tip, is that right? And then it stays there. What if the tip got full?
Carl	It will get fatter and fatter.
Researcher	The tip gets fatter and fatter. Could it get too fat?
Carl	It would go up and up.

John (USA)

Researcher	So instead of dropping the litter, what should we do with it?
John	Pick it up and put it in the trash.
Researcher	And when we pick it up and put it in the trash, do you know what happens to it. Where does it go?
John	Into the trash truck, and then it goes under the ground.

Researcher	Underneath the ground. How do you know about that?
John	My mom told me. . . . Recycling bottles . . .
Researcher	You know so much about trash. Well done. And do you know why we recycle bottles?
John	So we can use them again.
Researcher	Right. And why is it a good idea to use them again?
John	'Cos it's recycling stuff . . .
Researcher	And do you recycle things in your house?
John	We go to the store . . . and we get bags . . . we keep them under our sink . . . they're used for trash . . .
Researcher	So you use your bags over and over again?
John	Yes.
Researcher	Do you recycle paper?
John	Sure.
Researcher	And where does paper come from?
John	Trees.
Researcher	OK – so if we recycle paper, how is that helping the world?
John	Come back to you. The paper can come back, and we can use it again.

Kelly (USA)

Kelly	Yeah – they throw litter on the ground and in the water . . .
Researcher	Right.
Kelly	. . . and that's so bad.
Researcher	Right. What do you do with your litter?
Kelly	Er . . . you throw it in the trash can.
Researcher	Good girl. Do you know what happens to it when it's in the trash can?
Kelly	Er . . . The garbage man came and makes new stuff out of it.
Researcher	That's very good. Do you know what we call it when we make new stuff out of it?
Kelly	Er . . .
Researcher	There's a special word for it.
Kelly	It calls . . . recycling.
Researcher	Well done, Kelly. You know a lot about these things. How do you know all this?
Kelly	Mm . . . 'cos my daddy told me about it.
Researcher	And how do you know about recycling?
Kelly	Er . . . heard it on TV.
Researcher	OK. Is your family really good at recycling?
Kelly	Yeah.
Researcher	Do you know why recycling is very, very important?

Kelly	Uh-huh . . . 'Cos it makes . . . it can make new paper out of newspaper, that calls recycling.

Rachel (USA)

Researcher	What should we do with our trash?
Rachel	Um . . . recycle it . . .
Researcher	Recycle it – that's very good. Do you know what that means, Rachel?
Rachel	Um . . . use it back.
Researcher	That's right, use it back. What sort of things can we recycle?
Rachel	Um . . . cans . . . um . . . newspaper . . .
Researcher	Very good. Do you know why it's very important that we recycle things? Do you know why? Can you guess why?
Rachel	Because we don't want to waste things.
Researcher	Rachel, that's very, very good. How do you know about recycling?
Rachel	Because . . . I don't know – I just know it.

Stephanie (UK)

Researcher	What should we do with our rubbish?
Stephanie	Put it in the dustbin.
Researcher	That's right. Why shouldn't we throw rubbish on the ground?
Stephanie	Because the man that picks the rubbish has to come and pick it up.
Researcher	Why can't we leave it on the ground?
Stephanie	Because people would trip over it, wouldn't they?

Danielle (UK)

Researcher	What happens to the rubbish in the bin?
Danielle	You keep it in there.
Researcher	You keep it in the bin. And then does someone empty the bin?
Danielle	Yes.
Researcher	Who empties the bin?
Danielle	The bin man.
Researcher	The bin man. And do you know where the bin man takes it?
Danielle	To a rubbish man.
Researcher	Do you know what the rubbish man does with the rubbish?
Danielle	Puts it in a bin.

Eleanor (USA)

Eleanor	It can go for recycling . . . or in the rubbish bin.
Researcher	Well done. You know about recycling. What does that mean? Tell me about recycling.
Eleanor	You know, it's recycling . . . we have a recycling box out there.
Researcher	In school?
Eleanor	Yes.
Researcher	Oh, right. And is that a good thing to do?
Eleanor	Yes.
Researcher	Can you tell me why?
Eleanor	'Cos then we can use it again.
Researcher	Right. So that means that things you put in there, we can use them again. And do you know why that's very good, to use it again?
Eleanor	Because then they don't have to keep making some over and over again.

Analysis

Three categories of information emerged from the great wealth of data provided by the conversations:

- Details of the children's knowledge and understanding about people, places and environmental issues – including their accurate knowledge, gaps in knowledge and erroneous thinking. Such details provided substantial insight into the development of basic scientific concepts needed to understand the four issues being focused upon.
- Insights into the children's levels of awareness and concern for the world in which they are growing up, and problems which affect our planet.
- Details of the origins and sources of knowledge and concern in these pre-school children who had received no formal education programmes.

To consider the first of these categories, we see, for example, that the majority of children correctly associated trees with forests and animal and plant life. Some could identify specific animals and birds – cheetah (John and Daniel), orang-utan, chimpanzee, gorilla, jaguar (Stanley). Nicola could explain that wood makes paper and that trees have various uses for people; also that if trees are cut down, animals will lose their homes. John linked the use of trees with making fire and houses, and Nicola knew that many forests are located in South America. The majority of children interviewed could explain that if snow gets warm it melts. Eleanor explained that melting snow makes water (linking it with the sea) while Daniel provided the word 'evaporates', and Jocelyn explained that melting snow goes into bays, where water runs and people sit on the sand. A number of children, notably in California, had a relatively sophisticated under-standing of recycling waste materials. Eleanor linked this process with not making things 'over and over again', and Rachel clearly knew that we should not waste things in the world.

Alongside this array of accurate knowledge, we are provided with examples of false knowledge, gaps in knowledge and biased, stereotypical knowledge: John said that trees 'breathe air' but offered no further expla-nation of this; Stanley believed that rain forests are located in Spain and wasn't sure where disappearing snow goes to. Stephanie explained that the reason we shouldn't leave rubbish on the ground is in case people fall over it; Dean had the negative idea that forests are 'yuk', while Carl talked of snow going to the home of Santa Claus (he makes it) and rain forests being inhabited by soldiers who eat cabbage, potatoes, carrots, beefburgers, seafood and chips.

The data derived from these conversations thus provide insights into the development of basic concepts needed to understand our geographical world and related environmental issues. We are also provided with insights into the development of awareness of problems and concern for the world. Stanley talked of the need to protect trees and flowers; Jeffrey knew that wood can be wasted, and the majority of children explained that rubbish should be sensibly dealt with.

Sources of knowledge about the world were various, and included books, the media, parents, other relatives, and indeed a well-known 'happy food' restaurant.

The research project briefly outlined above aims to provide a detailed analysis of the categories of information illuminated by the data, to com-pare the knowledge and concern of children entering school with that of 6–7 year olds, thus illustrating aspects of development in geographical and environmental thinking during the first three years in school. The ultimate aim is to inform the development of curriculum materials and schemes of work for use with children during these early years of learning. In the context of this volume, preliminary analysis provides fascinating insights into 'the world of the 4 year old', which can illustrate and inform many of the practical issues addressed on forthcoming pages.

This chapter has therefore set the scene for discussion of appropriate learning tasks and methods of organising the curriculum for teaching and learning in geographical education.

Chapter 2

Geographical and environmental education

Structure, content and issues

STRUCTURE AND CONTENT

At the time of going to press, details of the content of the National Curriculum for geography are being reconsidered and rewritten. Whatever the final outcome, the 'essence' of its content – an inter-twining of the study of physical geography, human geography and environmental geography – will stand the test of time. The original National Curriculum Order provided a much-need rationale for teaching and learning in the subject; it also gave rise to a number of key issues which will be discussed. The core content of geography is comprised of five elements, these being:

- Geographical skills
- Places (near and far)
- Physical geography
- Human geography
- Environmental geography

These elements include the knowledge, skills and processes that should be taught. Progression is essential in the teaching of such knowledge, skills and processes, as exemplified by the National Curriculum framework:

Geographical skills

1 Enquiry should form an important part of pupils' work in geography in Key Stage 1. Work should be linked to pupils' own interests, experience and capabilities and should lead to investigations based on both fieldwork and classroom activities. Much of pupils' learning in Key Stage 1 should be based on direct experience, practical activities and exploration of the local area.

2 Pupils should be encouraged to ask geographical questions, for example, 'Why is this place like it is?', and to search for answers with the guidance of their teachers. Pupils should be given opportunities to use information technology (IT). They should be taught to:

- observe their surroundings, and examine pictures and pictorial maps of distant places, and use an increasing range of geographical terms, for example, hill, slope, river, road, house, shop, in describing what they see;
- identify similarities and differences between places, for example, in the ways land and buildings are used and in the life and work of people;
- select information that is relevant to a geographical study from material provided by the teacher, for example, select pictures of lakes, rivers and seas for a study of water.

3   Pupils should be taught to:

- follow directions, including the terms forwards and backwards, up and down, left and right, north, south, east and west;
- extract information from, and add it to, pictorial maps;
- draw around objects to make a plan, for example, mathematical shapes and household objects;
- make representations of actual or imaginary places, for example, their own bedroom, a treasure island;
- identify land and sea on maps and globes;
- follow a route on a map, for example, a map of the local area of the school produced by a teacher, another adult or a pupil;
- use pictures and photographs to identify features, for example, homes, railways, rivers, hills, and to find out about places;
- observe, describe and record the weather over a short period.

4   Pupils working towards level 3 should be taught to:

- use the eight points of the compass;
- make a map of a short route, showing main features in the correct order, for example, from home to the park;
- use letter and number co-ordinates to locate features on maps;
- locate their own position and identify features using a large-scale map;
- identify features on oblique aerial photographs.

(DES 1991)

A number of points of elaboration may be made concerning geography's core content:

> *Geographical Skills* – involves skills relating to the use of maps and fieldwork techniques.
> *Knowledge and Understanding of Places* – covers the features and similarities of and differences between places both near and further afield.

Physical Geography – covers weather and climate, rivers, seas and oceans; landforms; animals, plants and soils.

Human Geography – covers population, settlements, communications and movements, and economic activities.

Environmental Geography – covers the use and misuse of natural resources, the quality of different environments and considerations of conservation and management of environments and resources.

The designing of topics in geography is a matter for teachers' and schools' discretion.

So far this chapter has outlined and considered basic information about the content of geography. Let us also consider progress in creative interpretation of this. The report from the Office of Her Majesty's Chief Inspector of Schools (Ofsted 1993) concerned with the first year of implementation of the National Curriculum for Geography in Key Stages 1, 2 and 3 states that nearly three-quarters of the Key Stage 1 lessons inspected were based on the study of the home, the local area, the early development of map skills or the recording of weather conditions. Few lessons were based on the study of distant lands and their people. The best lessons were built on the direct experience of the pupils. 'These lessons were carefully planned and re-sourced, and the teachers had clear objectives related to the National Curriculum. The pupils, suitably guided by their teachers, were engaged in a variety of appropriate learning activities, maintained at a brisk pace' (Ofsted 1993). The report comments that some of the most effective lessons were focused on directions and routes, leading to a good understanding of map skills.

Regrettably, the same document informs the reader that while geography has strengthened its position in Key Stage 1 since the introduction of the National Curriculum, there is still too little geography in many schools. Much development is needed in terms of planning and organisation. 'In rather over half of those schools visited there were general guidelines that had some relevance to geography, but few had begun to detail requirements other than by outlining topics to be taught' (Ofsted 1993).

It is hoped that the forthcoming chapters in this book will be of assistance to teachers, both specialists and non-specialists alike, in their movement towards an overall curriculum plan for the teaching of geography within the early years curriculum, and towards creative and meaningful interpretation of national guidelines. The Ofsted Report (1993) recognises that some teachers find it difficult to translate the requirements of the Geography Order into a scheme of work or guidelines, partly because they are insecure in their own geographical understanding and partly because they still lack experience of curriculum planning. 'In several cases they relied too heavily on Attainment Targets to provide the structures which they required. In one 5–11 primary school, the scheme of work was no more than a photocopy of the Attainment Targets' (Ofsted 1993). I hope that subsequent chapters will assist in the translation of requirements.

It would be difficult, if not inappropriate, to pursue any discussion of learning experiences relating to the subject matter of geography without reference also to environmental education. These two components are inextricably linked in the early years curriculum, so their interrelationships must be considered.

While geography is a foundation subject, containing elements of environmental geography, environmental education exists in its own right as a cross-curricular theme intended to permeate the curriculum as a whole. As such, it shares with other themes 'the ability to foster discussion of questions of values and belief, . . . [cross-curricular themes] add to knowledge and understanding and . . . rely on practical activities, decision-making and the interrelationship of the individual and the community' (NCC 1990a).

It is recognised that cross-curricular themes have a substantial body of knowledge and understanding in their own right, while incorporating this 'values/belief' dimension. The aims, components and suggested content of environmental education are published in *Curriculum Guidance 7* (NCC 1990b). As an officially recognised cross-curricular element of the National Curriculum, it must be regarded as part of the entitlement of every school-aged pupil. It is not a statutory subject in its own right, but must be viewed as being complementary to, arising out of and permeating all the core and foundation subjects. In particular, it has a firm 'foothold' in geography, as we have seen. No single approach to the organisation of the curriculum or teaching methodology for environmental education is recommended. It is suggested that the combination of a variety of approaches is appropriate. In the early years of schooling, teaching through a series of subject-based or general topics lasting for various periods of time, combined with teaching through National Curriculum subject areas, is probably the best arrangement, which certainly fits alongside the teaching of geographically based topics. Topics may be subject-based, incorporating elements of environmental education, or the actual focus of a topic could be an issue deriving from the content of the theme. In this way, there is ample scope for cross-linking the content of geography and environmental education within suitable starting points for integrated development. Seven key areas of knowledge and understanding of the environment that should be covered in the curriculum are:

- climate;
- soils, rocks and minerals;
- water;

- materials and resources, including energy;
- plants and animals;
- people and their communities;
- buildings, industrialisation and waste.

These relate to a number of issues which have clear links with geography and other curriculum areas:

Topic	Issues
Climate	climatic effects on vegetation
	effects of pollution on climate, e.g. the ozone layer, greenhouse gases and acid deposition
Soil, rocks and minerals	resource limitation
	management of resources
	soil erosion, fertility and conservation
	the effects of extractive industries
Water	causes of water pollution
	water conservation
	problems of water supply
	effects of human activity on the hydrological cycle
Energy	fossil fuels as limited resource
	energy conservation
	pollution effects of energy use
Plants and animals	concern for other living things
	endangered species and conservation
	exploitation of wild populations of plants and animals
	destruction of natural habitats
People and communities	similarities and differences between people and how they use their environments
	population patterns and changes
	cultural aspects of the environment
	how societies in the past have influenced and been influenced by their environments
Buildings, industrialization and waste	impact of industrialization on the environment
	how and why the built environment has changed over time
	planning and design
	waste production and management of waste recycling
	appropriate technology for different conditions
	impact of new technologies on communities

(NCC 1990b)

Interpretation of these issues into topics and learning tasks is a matter for individual schools and teachers to pursue. What is certain is the need to incorporate within such plans the three essential interrelated components of environmental education, namely:

- education *about* the environment (i.e. basic knowledge and understanding of the environment);
- education *for* the environment (concerned with values, attitudes and positive action for the environment);
- education *in* or *through* the environment (i.e. using the environment as a resource with emphasis on enquiry and investigation and pupils' first-hand experiences).

These three components are inextricably linked, and are thus essential to the planning of educational programmes and tasks at all levels, including whole-school curriculum plans and specific programmes of work/activities for individuals and class groups. Part of the planning process should take account of the need to help learners understand the interrelationships that exist among the three elements.

An alternative or complementary way of interpreting this structure is to suggest that every child has a basic entitlement in environmental education. A statement of proposed entitlement of pupils in environmental education was prepared in England by the group convened by the NCC to examine this theme and prepare documentation for *Curriculum Guidance 7*. The entitlement formed part of a collection of key papers (unpublished) circulated widely for consultation and response. It suggests that a pupil's learning should be founded on knowledge, understanding and skills. A summary follows. It is clear that the critical time for commencing an implementation of this entitlement is in the primary phase; indeed, in the early years.

By the age of 16 all pupils should have had educational experiences, which range from local to global in scale, and which enable them to:

1 understand the natural processes that take place in the environment, including the ecological principles and relationships that exist;
2 understand that human lives and livelihoods are totally dependent on the processes, relationships and resources that exist in the environment;
3 be aware of the impact of human activities on the environment including planning and design, to understand the processes by which communities organise themselves, initiate and cope with change; to appreciate that these are affected by personal, economic, technological, social, aesthetic, political, cultural, ethical and spiritual considerations;
4 be competent in a range of skills which help them to appreciate and

enjoy, communicate ideas and participate in the decision-making processes which shape the environment;

5 view, evaluate, interpret and experience their surroundings critically so that a balanced appreciation can be reached;

6 have insights into a range of environments and cultures, both past and present, to include an understanding of the ways in which different cultural groups perceive and interact with their environment;

7 understand the conflict that may arise over environmental issues, particularly in relation to the use of resources, and to consider alternative ways to resolve such conflicts;

8 be aware of the interdependence of communities and nations and some of the environmental consequences and opportunities of those relationships;

9 be aware that the current state of the environment has resulted from past decisions to which they made a contribution;

10 identify their own level of commitment towards the care of the environment.

Underpinning this entitlement is a clear emphasis on values and attitudes. Indeed a critical component of cross-curricular issues in general is surely their ability to promote discussion of questions of values, beliefs and personal decision-making as a response to interaction with the environment. The entitlement can also be seen to have clear links with geographical education, with its emphasis on natural processes, human activity and range of environments and cultures.

This entitlement incorporates strands which interrelate with other areas of the curriculum. These strands include:

1 *Knowledge, understanding and attitudes*
(a) Knowledge about the environment at a variety of levels, ranging from local to global.
(b) Knowledge and understanding of environmental issues at a variety of levels, ranging from local to global.
(c) Knowledge of alternative attitudes and approaches to environmental issues and the value systems underlying such attitudes and approaches.

2 *Skills*
(a) Finding out about the environment, either directly in or through the environment or by using secondary resources.
(b) Communicating:
    (i) knowledge about the environment to others;
    (ii) both the pupils' own and alternative attitudes to environmental issues, to include justification for the attitudes or approaches advanced.
(c) Involvement in decision-making.

The success of incorporating worthwhile programmes of environmental education into the school curriculum is thus dependent upon the inclusion of these strands within the over-arching threefold framework outlined above and taking account of meaningful integration with other subject areas through carefully structured cross-curricular tasks. Figure 2.1 provides a diagrammatic representation of this framework for planning.

Discussion now returns to the content of geography, and attempts to tease out the common ground between these two curriculum areas. The element of geographical skills involves both the use of maps and fieldwork. Clearly this incorporates the 'essence' of environmental education which is learning, from first hand, practical 'field' experiences. As this element is not intended to be taught in isolation, but to be related to the content of the others, in many instances it can overlap with and incorporate the seven topics of environmental education. Knowledge and understanding of places involves learning about a variety of scales of place. Individual schools and teachers are to select places for study. Once again, this is totally

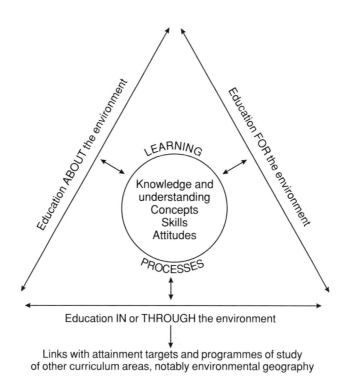

Figure 2.1   Interrelated components of environmental education

in line with the requirements of environmental education which are to incorporate learning in, through and about the environment, using both the immediate locality and places further afield. The components of physical geography clearly demonstrate overlap with education about the environment, notably the topics of climate; soil, rocks and minerals; water; and plants and animals. The components of human geography are inter-linked with the environmental education content areas of people, their communities and buildings, industrialisation and waste. Finally, environmental geography is intimately linked with the theme of environmental education. It is concerned with issues and beliefs as well as knowledge relating to planet Earth. It incorporates not only elements of learning about the environment, but also the critical third component of environmental education, that of learning *for* the environment, concerned with values, attitudes and positive action.

In summary, therefore, geographical learning in the early years involves the structured content of a foundation subject which has a distinct integrity and identifiable content of its own, while maintaining meaningful and well-planned links with a cross-curricular theme.

ISSUES

The content and interrelationships of these two areas of knowledge, under-standing and skills on the curriculum map raise a number of issues relating to the development of children's thinking and organisation of teaching and learning in these areas.

Such issues permeate this book as a whole, but several will now be highlighted before being elaborated upon in the context of practical examples in this and subsequent chapters. Issues raised are in no particular order of priority. Neither do they form a comprehensive list. They do, however, provide a focus for further discussion on the design and im-plementation of policies and programmes of work in geographical and environmental education in the first three years in school.

The first issue relates to the use of first-hand experiences in the local environment which are essential starting points for the development of classroom tasks. Such organised local experiences will capitalise upon children's spontaneous experiences and previously acquired knowledge of the world around them, while developing this understanding through carefully structured, progressive activities.

Having emphasised the importance of using the locality, a second issue focuses on the need to go beyond the immediate environment, to challenge parochialism and develop children's awareness and understanding of places farther afield. It seems that traditionally schools have failed to address aspects of the geography of distant lands. In their survey, *Aspects of the Primary Curriculum. The Teaching and Learning of History and Geography* (1989), HMI make the following criticism:

> Work related to other places in the British Isles and the world was limited. The almost total absence of a national and world dimension to the work in many cases highlighted the need for schools to consider a broader perspective.

(DES 1989)

This issue is taken up for discussion at a later stage in the context of case studies relating to teaching about distant lands.

Third, teachers need to consider the central role of fieldwork and the process and skills of enquiry in teaching and learning. These are an integral part of any successful topics/schemes of work and progressive attainment in fieldwork and environmental enquiry skills should be recognised as an essential component of geography teaching. Geographical education in the early years requires a wide variety of teaching methods with great emphasis on the enquiry approach. Giving knowledge directly, creative activities, questioning, group and individual tasks, information technology, use of stories/drama/role play, books, maps and other secondary resources all have their part to play. Yet if asked to highlight the most important ingredient of teaching and learning which characterises well-executed geographical schemes, planned fieldwork tasks would be the answer. To many this no doubt conjures up images of mountains, trails, walking boots and backpacks, but no child in school is too young to have a wide variety of learning tasks set in the outdoors, beginning, of course, with the school playground and its immediate environment. All work outside the classroom both uses and extends the world with which young children are familiar, and if trips further afield into the neighbourhood and beyond can be organised, so much the better. Ideally, year 2 children should have opportunities to visit and investigate contrasting environments, perhaps a farm if the school is in an inner-city area, or a shopping complex/town centre if the school is in a rural community. The inclusion of fieldwork activities should certainly be addressed in all school curriculum plans and policy documents for the teaching of geography.

A fourth issue is a focus in teaching and learning on the concepts of space and place, i.e. on the nature and dynamics of places, spatial relationships in the environment, the human dimension, and environmental impacts and issues. This focus incorporates the all-important dimension of attitude development and the question of making informed value judgements about places.

A fifth issue concerns the context for the planning of teaching and learning in geography. Organisation needs to take account of the context of geographical and environmental learning, that is, the relationship with and the interconnectedness of these areas to other aspects of the curriculum –

links should not only be recognised and respected but planned for. Again HMI have made serious criticism of geographical work surveyed.

> Overall standards of work in geography were very disappointing . . . geography was most frequently taught in association with other areas of the curriculum . . . the amount of time allocated to work with a geographical component was rarely adequate . . . in most schools, there was a tendency for geography to lose its distinctive contribution and to become a vehicle for practising skills related to language and art. In contrast the mathematical and scientific potential of geographical skills, in the case of map work and weather observations, was only occasionally exploited.
>
> (DES 1989)

Geography and environmental education can clearly be *supportive* of learning in other areas, and can provide the unifying element in an integrated topic. Furthermore, they can make a *distinctive* contribution to children's learning – particularly in the area of spatial knowledge. Both of these roles – the supportive and the distinctive – cannot be left to chance and must be planned for.

Finally, all schools must address the issue of the resources needed to interpret and develop geographical schemes into worthwhile learning tasks. HMI have commented on the relatively low status which has traditionally been given to this area of the curriculum, reflected in a poor level or almost complete absence of resources in many schools.

> In few schools did the resources reflect the multi-ethnic composition of either the school or society in terms of books, maps, audio and visual materials. There was some evidence to suggest that schools which were most successful in teaching geography also possessed a broad range of resources.
>
> (DES 1989)

This significant matter is addressed extensively in this volume, notably in Chapter 7, but it is implicitly addressed in the context of a number of the case studies.

Rather than continue a discussion in abstract, these and other related issues will be considered in context, with specific examples of content. Attention is turned in the first instance to an example of environmental geography in practice, which illustrates the close links between these two subject areas.

Mrs King's class of 7 year olds spent a school term focusing attention on the theme of 'Woodlands'. A series of visits was made to a woodland area, and every opportunity taken to engage the children in first-hand experiences and skills of fieldwork in this habitat. Practical investigatory work was at the forefront of learning. Back in the classroom, these experiences were followed up through integrated topic work, with a discernible core of environmental geography linked to science. The children were helped to identify the various different types of tree observed in the field with the aid of simple keys and photographs. The trees and their leaves were sketched, and samples of leaves and fruits were taken to the classroom so that leaf prints and sketches could be made. The children wrote creative accounts of the vibrant colours seen in the woodland, and more factual sentences about chronology of change as the autumn progressed. Attention was paid to accuracy and detail as well as imaginative and creative interpretation:

> 'Now, children, look carefully at the leaves you collected. How many ways are they different from each other? Let's make a list.'
> 'Little leaves and big leaves, miss.'
> 'Give me one word that means little and big. The leaves are different . . .?'
> 'Sizes, miss.'
> 'Yes, good boy, Mohammed. Who can spell the word "size"? Tell me another way leaves are different. Tajinder?'
> 'Shapes – some are wide and some are narrow. Some are one big leaf and some look like they're made up of different bits stuck together.'
> 'That's right . . . can you tell me another word that means "wide" children?'

> [Discussion led to the introduction of the name and the classification 'broadleaf' and leaves were put into sets of broadleaves and conifers.]

> 'Colours are different too, miss. There are green ones and yellowy ones and most of them are a mixture.'
> 'I know another way they're different. The edges of the leaves are different – some have jagged edges, and others are straight.'

As continuation of the follow-up to first-hand experiences of the woodland, Mrs King organised various games and classification activities. A tray was set out, containing various different leaves to encourage greater facility in identifying specimens from holly, yew, oak, pine, privet, laurel, beech, larch, sweet chestnut and so on, and then classifying each as either broadleaf or conifer. Posters and sets of commercial cards on the theme of trees and woodlands were available as secondary resource material to reinforce and assist the process. A great deal of emphasis was placed on scientific accuracy, facts and information – trees and leaves, fruits and seeds were identified and classified, and their habits and characteristics discussed and investigated in the field. Field experiences were then linked to human geography.

The value of trees and their usefulness to human life were considered, and samples of numerous woods were displayed alongside a collection of library books on the subject of wood and trees and photographs of important things in our lives made of wood. The more able children were given research tasks using these resources to discover which parts of the world each piece of wood came from.

A number of different issues and sub-topics were covered, including a comparison of differing woodland areas (temperate and tropical) throughout the world and the key conservation issue of decline of the world's tropical rain forests. Mrs King incorporated a video recording about 'Pauline's family in Borneo', in order to compare and contrast life styles in other parts of the world with the children's own urban surroundings. The pupils investigated the difference in diets, homes and clothing, how food and drink was obtained, and the cost of food in both places. The results were listed, discussed, compared and analysed. Speculation and imagination paralleled accuracy and interpretation of facts. Material contained within the recording lent itself to further factual writing and a great deal of creative art and craft work and imaginative writing ensued.

The children were intrigued by a life style of hunting and living off the land. 'Wish I could live over there,' sighed Abdul. 'I'd have lots of exciting adventures in the jungle.' Further discussion led to opportunities for drama and creative role play. Tropical rain forest scenes were acted out, depicting their wide variety of colourful life, restless atmosphere and sound effects. Vivid accounts accompanied this involvement, describing how different everyday activities would be in Borneo compared with life in an inner city in the UK.

In many ways, the further topic undertaken by Mrs King's pupils followed on from this comparison of rain forest life with that nearer home. A comparison of Borneo and Birmingham led to an investigation into 'wildlife in the city', largely as a response to those children who considered it a barren urban desert, devoid of the colour and excitement of more 'exotic' places. Fieldwork visits to farm and woodland once again provided a focus of first-hand experiences and practical investigations. The children undertook searches on land, in the air and in the water to discover how many species of wildlife inhabited the urban area of the centre. Bird-watching, pond-dipping and land searches of the various habitats led to a good deal of experience in identifying animal life. The activity aroused considerable excitement among the groups of learners, who soon became accustomed to handling petri dishes, magnifying containers, sweep nets, pooters and identification trays.

'Coo, miss, I feel like Sherlock Holmes doing this!'

[New words readily enter the children's vocabulary.]

'Who can tell me what we call a creature without a backbone?'
'A . . . invertebrate, miss?'

[The various groups of invertebrates were named, and the children's catches were then examined, counted and classified.]

'This creature has . . . how many legs?'

'Eight, miss.'

'So it belongs to . . . which group of invertebrates?'

'Arachnids.'

Results of surveys were listed formally and graphs were drawn to illustrate and compare the numbers of creatures found in various classes. One group of interested children spent some time researching the life history and habits of common invertebrates and writing illustrated accounts of these. The whole class drew and painted pictures which were incorporated into a giant panoramic landscape running the length of the classroom wall. Indeed as the year continued, Mrs King involved all the children in contributing towards interactive displays for both classroom and school hallways.

Once again, this topic was skilfully linked to learning about distant environments. Photographs of non-indigenous invertebrates (e.g. giant hissing cockroaches, giant millepedes, African land snails) were studied and a cage of locusts was set up in the classroom for detailed observation and investigatory work. Research was done into the countries of origin of locusts, and the climatic conditions necessary for them to flourish. Much discussion centred around the need to keep locusts in a heated cage, and the (un)likelihood of their survival in our own country because of the nature of our climate. Stories written about 'My Life as a Locust' encouraged empathy with warmer lands and led to reading and discussion of Bible stories involving a locust plague.

This example represents good practice in terms of establishing meaningful links between the core content of geography and components of environmental education. The whole topic was based on fieldwork and skills of practical enquiry. It incorporated all five elements of geographical content. Furthermore, the topic identified only those other areas of the curriculum with which useful and meaningful links for integration could be achieved, notably science. Environmental education therefore served its planned purpose of providing that cross-curricular link between geography and science.

Attainment targets of these areas and the formal entitlement of environmental education were at the forefront of planning; for example, the children's work on tropical rain forests enabled them to have insights into other cultures and an increased understanding of the ways in which different cultural groups perceive and interact with their environment. Attitudes, values and beliefs were recognised as key elements of the learning process. Table 2.1 represents diagrammatically an extract from a simplified version of the planning model used, and is not intended to be comprehensive. Examples of entries are given in each column.

In summary, this example has demonstrated ways in which practical

Table 2.1 Extract from a planning model

Topic	Education about the environment	Education for and in the environment	Links with other curriculum areas*	Cross-curricular skills
Woodland past and present	Concern for trees as living things	Visit to woodland, study of trees and leaves in their natural habitat	Science Geography	Observation
	Endangered species and conservation	Animal and plant life associated with trees	Geography Technology	Problem-solving Study
	Exploitation of populations of plants and animals	Sub-topic on trees in distant lands (using secondary resources)	Mathematics Geography	Communica-tion
	Destruction of natural habitats, especially tropical rain forests	Development of care and 'caretaker ethic'	English Geography	Participation Personal and social

* Specific cross-referencing with attainments targets and programmes of study for the core and foundation subjects of the National Curriculum was documented.

links can be made between the two subject areas of geography and environmental education. It has also exemplified a number of the key issues arising out of the National Curriculum documentation for geography, notably the need for an emphasis on fieldwork and investigatory tasks in the locality, and the need to challenge this parochialism and find tangible ways of teaching and learning about distant lands.

Attention is now turned to a more detailed discussion of the crucial tasks of planning and organising geographical education in the first three years in school.

Chapter 3

Planning and organisation

PLANNING IN CONTEXT: BUILDING ON WHAT THE LEARNER KNOWS

Planning for the teaching of geography, like all subjects, must inevitably incorporate an understanding of what the learners already know, that is, what they are bringing to the learning situation, and the related ability of a teacher to find this out and to develop it. Perhaps the appropriate place to pursue this discussion is in the context of learning in action in classrooms. It is emphasised that all classroom discussions and descriptions used in this volume are for the purpose of illustrating particular points or issues. They do not necessarily represent examples of 'ideal' or recommended practice – just day-to-day life in schools. Their strengths, and in some cases their weaknesses, are highlighted. Most important, they locate the theoretical and research framework in the real and complex world of children's lives.

Consider the following three examples of geographical learning in action, and the conversations taking place within them.

Mrs Friend's class

Four 5–6 year old children are attempting to reorganise parts of a model village back on to the base that it had occupied the day before. Mrs Friend aims to use this everyday 'play' situation as an opportunity to develop basic geographical concepts concerned with the location of objects in space, and scaled down versions of reality.

Teacher	What's happened to the model? We don't have a village any more. Can you put it back together again?
Simon	The real village?
Teacher	The one we have in our classroom. Why isn't it a real one?
Simon	'Cos the houses are tiny.
Teacher	They're not as big as our houses, are they? Can you think why not?
Fiona	You can't fit a house in a school!

Teacher	Are these houses the same shape as ours? Stand here and look at the top of them . . . what shape do you see when you look down on them?
Jane	Square.
Carlton	Rectangles.

(Children continue discussing the 'bird's eye view' with interventions by their teacher.)

Teacher	Let's make the village like it was yesterday.
Fiona	What shall we start with?
Carlton	The church.
Simon	I know where the church goes.
Jane	Where?
Simon	There. Over there – by where the trees used to be.
Carlton	Why there?
Simon	'Cos that's where the graveyard is. You have to have a church by the side of the graveyard.
Fiona	Here?
Simon	No. Put it on the other side – that's where the gate is.
Fiona	Right. The church goes – there.
Carlton	Get the houses.
Simon	There's lots of them.
Fiona	They all go round the pond.
Carlton	Yes.
Jane	There was a house next to the church.
Simon	This one?
Carlton	The red one?
Simon	Blue one.
Carlton	And the green one went there.
Jane	I can't remember.
Fiona	I think it was blue. Yes, it was.
Simon	The red house was on the end. The blue one was in between the red house and the church.
Carlton	Let's put the red house on the end . . .
Jane	And the blue house next to the red one.
Fiona	Then the church is next door to the blue one.
Jane	Looks right.
Fiona	Yes, I think so.
Simon	What's left, then?
Carlton	The shop.
Jane	And another house.
Fiona	A green one.
Carlton	The shop was at the other end.

Fiona	On the end?
Simon	Yes. I think it goes there – opposite the red one and the blue one.
Carlton	There's only the green one left.
Jane	Where does that go?
Simon	There.
Fiona	In between the shop and the trees.
Jane	There?
Carlton	Yes.
Jane	Are you sure?
Fiona	Yes.
Simon	How do you know?
Fiona	I just know.
Teacher	The house is the same colour as the trees next to it.

Miss Reynolds' class

A group of children aged 6–7 are pursuing their studies in a topic on tropical rain forests. They are making collage pictures of the forest, and talking about what it would be like to visit a rain forest. This activity is but one of a wide range of practical tasks the children undertake which link various curriculum areas. While geographical education is the core of their work, a great deal of language, art, music, mathematics and science is also incorporated. In this particular lesson, geography leads to some relevant and exciting art and craft work. Its production generates much discussion. The teacher's aim is to establish meaningful links between concepts in science and geography, through the use of art. At the same time she is concerned with establishing levels and accuracy of existing knowledge.

Jed	Wonder what it would be like . . .
Cheryl	What?
Jed	Living in a rain forest.
Teacher	Think of some words to describe the air.
Sebastian	Hot.
Cheryl	And wet, too.
Annette	Must be like a steamy bathroom.
Sebastian	More like a shower. One you've always left running.
Jed	All the time. That's why everything grows so high. Like the trees, see?
Annette	They look as if they're stretching up to touch the sky.
Teacher	Why do they stretch so tall?
Cheryl	Finding the sun, that's why.
Jed	Look how big they are. Taller than telegraph poles. I bet it would take all day to climb one.

Teacher	Would it get lighter or darker as you climbed?
Sebastian	It's dark at the top.
Annette	But the leaves are spreading out to find the sunshine. That's why the light in the forest shines down all greeny-yellowy.
Jed	It's sunny outside the forest, but sort of shadowy inside.
Teacher	Can you try and show the shadows in your pictures?
Cheryl	There's still lots of colours, though.
Annette	Yes – red and yellow and green and blue, from all the wildlife you can find.
Jed	Like this parrot I'm painting.
Annette	Parrots don't have colours like those.
Jed	How do you know?
Annette	Well, I've never seen parrots like that.
Sebastian	Yes, but you've never been in a rain forest, have you?
Annette	No.
Sebastian	Well, then. How do you know there won't be parrots this colour in there?
Teacher	Our books help us to understand what colour they are.
Jed	We could find all sorts of strange, new birds there.
Cheryl	Yeah. There must be loads of flowers that we've never seen, 'cos they won't grow anywhere else.
Jed	And lots of tropical plants, too. Just like a jungle.
Cheryl	And fruits. Juicy fruits. Enormous things.
Sebastian	I fancy swinging through the trees on those trailing creepers, like Tarzan. That must be like flying.
Annette	Lots of animals live there too.
Jed	Jaguars. Tree frogs. And monkeys.
Cheryl	I think the monkeys would be my favourites.
Sebastian	The big ones, or the little ones?
Cheryl	What do you mean?
Sebastian	Well, there might be big monkeys like gorillas, and little ones. Chimpanzees.
Annette	I think I'd like the little ones best. They make me laugh. The gorillas would frighten me.
Jed	Not as much as the snakes, I bet. Great big pythons and boa constrictors all in the grass. Slithering about. They might kill you.
Teacher	But have you ever thought that they might be killed themselves?
Cheryl	They may kill insects. Butterflies in all the colours you can think of.
Sebastian	And spiders. And lizards.
Jed	I bet there are lots of funny creepy crawlies out there. All huge and furry.

Annette	All making squeaky noises at night. I saw them on the telly.
Sebastian	Ever so exciting. And spooky.
Jed	A rain forest must be a really noisy place. Everything screeching and squawking and flapping about.
Teacher	We can write about the noises of the forest.
Cheryl	All the roaring and growling from the wild animals.
Annette	And chattering.
Jed	Must be a bit like a big city, I should think.
Annette	How do you mean? It's a forest, not a city.
Jed	Well, the city's always full of noise. All the traffic all day. I should think the rain forest is like that, but there's animals there instead of people. And instead of flats, they have great big trees.
Sebastian	I'd love to be an explorer. I'd find new creatures and bring them back home again. I'd keep them safe as pets. I'm going to write about being an explorer and discovering a magic grub. Bright purple and enormous, and it hangs on twigs.

Mr Jones' class

Some 7–8 year olds are doing group activities to learn about the use of scale. They have already done some work on drawing round familiar objects on a piece of paper. Now they encounter things that are too big to fit the paper.

Teacher	We've drawn round lots of different things on our paper. Now, let's have a little problem to solve.
Andrew	What sort of problem?
Teacher	Well, all the objects you've drawn round so far fit on to the paper. Now I want you to draw your desk lid on this piece of paper.
Anne	But we can't, sir.
Joyce	It won't fit on.
Teacher	That's the problem I want you to solve. How can we draw big things on a smaller piece of paper?
Emily	Get a bigger piece of paper – then it would fit on all right.
Teacher	Yes, but what about bigger shapes? Like a frieze board, or a wall.
Joyce	Or an elephant.
Martin	We can't just keep on getting bigger bits of paper.
Andrew	If we wanted to draw the playground, we couldn't find a piece of paper that big.
Teacher	So what are we going to do?
Anne	If we can't make the paper bigger, draw the picture smaller. Then it'll fit on the paper.

Martin	Yes, that should do it.
Andrew	They do that in books, don't they, sir? Lots of book pictures have big things in them.
Teacher	Yes, Andrew, they do. In fact, if you look round the classroom, you'll find that someone has managed to draw the whole world in quite a small way.
Joyce	Where?
Emily	I can't see anything.
Martin	I can – over there. Look.
Andrew	It's a globe. It's got all the countries of the world on, hasn't it, sir?
Teacher	Yes.
Martin	How do they know what size the different countries are?
Andrew	I expect someone goes round and measures them.
Joyce	And then they have to make them small enough to fit on the globe.
Emily	Maps are like pictures, sir. They have sort of pictures of places on, don't they?
Teacher	That's right, Emily. Sometimes they show the whole country, and sometimes they might just show the streets of a town or a city.
Andrew	My dad's got a book with maps in it. It helps him to find his way round when he's driving his lorry.
Martin	How do they know what size to make the streets?
Andrew	Like with globes, I suppose – you have to measure things and then make them smaller . . .
Anne	To fit on the paper.
Emily	I suppose so.
Andrew	My brother's got Concorde in his bedroom.
Anne	He can't have – it wouldn't fit.
Andrew	It's not a real one – he made it out of a kit. It looks just like the real thing.
Emily	Somebody must have measured a real Concorde and then made it like a model.
Martin	So if we want to draw our desk lids, we'll have to measure how long it is . . .
Emily	And how wide it is.
Martin	And then make it smaller. Shorten it.
Andrew	How much by?
Anne	It'll have to be the same on each side, or it won't look right.
Teacher	Why not try to draw it about half its normal size? Measure each side, and then think of what half is.
Martin	Right. You measure how long it is, Andrew. Then we'll see how wide it is.

Anne	And then I'll halve it for you.
Andrew	I'll try and measure the inkwell.
Emily	What for?
Andrew	If we draw the desk smaller than it really is, we'll have to make the inkwell smaller too. If we draw it full size, it will look as big as a dustbin.
Martin	And that won't look right.

These three classroom scenes illustrate situations wherein young learners' complex processes of learning are engaged. Geographical education is taking place within their own familiar environment, and the knowledge, understanding, skills and concepts of geography are developed in the context of pupils' individual potential, prior experience and natural curiosity. The teacher's role, however, is crucial in each situation. He/she acts as facilitator and enabler of this development and as director/provider of tasks which nurture it.

Analysis of the conversation taking place in Mrs Friend's class leaves us with little doubt that the children are building upon the natural experiences and prior knowledge which they bring into the classroom. This experience is reflected by their teacher in specific and relevant tasks in which the children are engaging themselves. While the model is discussed and organised, key concepts and skills of mapwork and graphicacy are reinforced. The buildings are being linked together in physical space and in the children's minds – an important mapwork concept. The learners are familiarising themselves with the idea that a plan (or map) is a representation of space occupied by objects depicted in plan form and of the spatial relationship between them. The interventions by their teacher drawing attention to the 'view from above' are planned to assist this familiarisation. The children are surrounded in this activity by first-hand experiences of the concept of scale – without conscious realisation and discussion of the fact. The teacher uses this opportunity to pose relevant questions – why are these houses smaller than the ones we really live in? – a promotion of valuable geographical discussion, linked to the general development of vocabulary and conversation about everyday things. Without doubt, this simple 'play' activity of reassembling a model is sound early years geographical education, affording practice in recording locations, and development of the vocabulary of graphicacy, including 'opposite', 'in front of', 'by the side of', 'behind', 'next to', 'right' and 'left'. Such vocabulary is linked to an understanding of direction and the more advanced concepts involving grids, co-ordinates and recording specific locations to which the children will progress in their learning. Mrs Friend is successfully allowing natural conversation and experiential learning to take place, while steering the task and its related discussion towards specific elements of geographical education. Knowledge and skills are developed which are entirely appropriate for such young learners' stage of conceptual development.

In Miss Reynolds' classroom, tasks are organised through the topic-work approach – in this example, a topic which clearly has geographical education as a discernible core of content. Conversation illustrates existing subject knowledge which children bring to their task: rain forests are hot and wet, the trees are very tall . . . they need the sun . . . they are home for a wide range of colourful and exciting things – birds, animals, insects and flowers. Snatches of conversation reveal a wealth of existing concepts and ideas, no doubt established as a result of previous work done on the topic and exposure to views of life in rain forests presented by the media, books and conversations with others. The classroom scene certainly illuminates existing subject knowledge. It also demonstrates the erroneous or incomplete nature of this knowledge which exists in the 'world inside children's minds'.

Young pupils' background knowledge of distant environments is an important consideration when planning further work on them, and perhaps the word 'knowledge' is not the most accurate one to use, as Chapter 1 suggests. Children have ever-increasing incidental contact with places around the world – through personal contacts, package holidays, films, television and other media. All these are powerful influences. Inevitably children build up a 'mental map' or image of foreign places which to a large extent may be blurred or false. Various reports contribute to our awareness of the blurred knowledge of the distant world contained within children's minds, and draw attention to research findings on both the quantity and quality of information which children possess of places beyond their immediate environment. The research discussed in Chapter 1 which is in progress at Durham and Stanford Universities (Palmer 1992b, 1993) illustrates a range of blurred or false concepts commonly held by 4 year old children. For example:

- If snow at the North Pole melts, it moves to somewhere else such as Alaska.
- If the Arctic and Antarctic weather becomes warmer, the snow gets hot.
- People cannot live in rain forests because it is too dark.
- Rain forest people live in the trees like the monkeys.
- Melting snow goes to Heaven.

As well as factual errors, attention is drawn to the dangers of stereotyping and ethnocentricity that result from media reports. Chapter 1 also referred to the research of Storm (1984) who reports a word association test with primary age children in Wokingham, England. Results showed that the words most commonly associated with Africa were those which conjure up images of the exotic and the excitement of the land, far removed from the realities of many parts of Africa today. Miss Reynolds' classroom is an interesting parallel. Her young learners discuss the colourful and exotic aspects of tropical rain forests – large, juicy fruits, colourful parrots, beautiful butterflies and exciting animals. They speculate on swinging through the trees like Tarzan – images probably reinforced by books and films, yet far removed from the realities of a rain forest's destruction, soil erosion and the frequent plight of native peoples. Misinformation and stereotyping can so often arise and be reinforced, perhaps by the teacher's own genuine ignorance of particular facts about a place. A paradoxical argument could be pursued. How important is it for a teacher to build upon a learner's existing knowledge and experiences? Yet to a certain extent these may be incomplete, erroneous or biased. Thus a teacher's task is to establish the pupils' existing knowledge base – to find out what is already known and understood, and also to have some idea of what is not known or partially understood.

In the first two of these classrooms we see evidence of teachers using existing understanding and everyday experiences to enhance future learning tasks. Mrs Friend approached this through everyday 'play' activities, and Miss Reynolds through a structured topic. In Mr Jones' classroom, the children's experience and learning is organised through the subject matter of geography itself. Tasks are planned which will lead to an understanding of scale, a key concept in graphicacy. The teacher sees his role as progressing this understanding, enabling the children's own practical work and spontaneous ideas, while organising certain experiences so that logical connections are made between elements of subject matter. Learning is an organised event – and the teacher provides appropriate ways of introducing the pupils to strategies that will reinforce their discoveries and aid their progressive understanding of the content of geography.

Thus we see three very different examples of approaching learning in geography – one which capitalises on natural or everyday objects and experiences, one which develops prior experience by relying on the integration of subject matter through a cross-curricular topic, and one which introduces specific knowledge in its own right. All result in achievement in learning and represent 'good practice' in geographical education. All three are appropriate methods of developing prior experience into worthwhile learning tasks, and take account of a key issue in planning which is that context is crucial for the facilitation of learning. In each classroom, pupils did not learn arbitrary facts with no relevance to their lives. The goals of learning made sense to the learners, so giving meaning to the learned material.

A number of general conclusions may be drawn from and supported by these examples. First and foremost, a great deal of prior geographical knowledge is brought to a learning situation. Young children coming into school are actually good at learning. They make persistent attempts to make sense of their complex world. Rather than perceiving children as 'blank slates', a teacher ought to recognise the learners' existing adaptations to their environment. He or she should in some way 'tap into' their predispositions rather than attempt to teach arbitrary associations which are not mapped on to the constraints of experience brought to the classroom.

Desforges (1989) elaborates upon a discussion of research findings which suggest that the majority of young children are good at learning (even though they may not regularly engage themselves in the process). A considerable literature deriving from research evidence provides a commentary on learning before school, i.e. that which children 'bring with them' into the classroom. Attention is drawn, for example, to studies of emergent literacy (Hall 1987). Margaret Clark (1976) demonstrated that some pre-school children make remarkable progress in learning to read without support from parents. Parallel studies derive from the subject areas of mathematics: Gellman and Gallistel (1978) show how young children can conserve small numbers, Carpenter et al. (1982) demonstrate that pre-school children can solve word problems or the addition and subtraction of small numbers, and Hughes (1986) concludes that young children understand small numbers and number operations when presented in the form of games.

These examples are selected from many studies in the areas of numeracy and literacy. Current research, as discussed in Chapter 1 (Palmer 1992b, 1993), highlights early learning in the area of emerging environmental cognition. All confirm that pre-school children are remarkably efficient learners, and bring a range of skills, concepts and subject knowledge as background to the teacher's task – even if such knowledge is not entirely accurate or complete.

The task of planning for learning therefore involves designing experiences which build upon children's existing knowledge of the world around them. This can be done in a number of ways, as the classroom scenarios have shown.

If teachers are to pursue this complex task of ascertaining children's prior knowledge and building upon it, two conditions seem essential to the process. First, they must have an adequate understanding of the subject matter of geography: it seems clear that if teachers do not have an adequate grasp of knowledge of a subject it is impossible for them to tease out that subject's underlying principles and intellectual integrity in order to structure learning tasks and progressive activities which take account of these. The teaching task involves identifying clear lines of progression within the subject. Second, they must have the ability to organise suitable learning tasks which children can engage with in the appropriate context and at the appropriate time.

Two general points must be made about learning tasks: they should be both purposeful in the eyes of the learner and relevant to his or her experiences, and should also have the potential for progression or expansion in order to facilitate further learning in geography or a related curriculum area. The teacher's own task involves making judgements about such relevance and potential, perhaps using the following checklist of questions:

Are tasks

- Purposeful?
- Relevant?
- Rigorous?
- Challenging?
- Sequential?

From general characteristics, planning may then take account of more specific analysis of types of task in the context of adequate coverage of the geography curriculum.

Task planned should enable pupils to:

- consolidate and practise existing geographical knowledge/skills;
- build upon such existing understanding;
- achieve clearly identified progression within the subject;
- make meaningful intellectual links between geography and other subject areas;
- engage in imaginative thinking and creative problem-solving.

The three geography classroom situations described above provide examples of teaching which aims to take account of setting tasks matched to the learners' ability, experience and interest. Furthermore, they illuminate three possible ways of facilitating further learning. Effective teaching and learning in geography may well incorporate all three of these approaches, extended into the provision of a wide range of appropriate tasks.

PLANNING IN ACTION: ENVIRONMENTAL GEOGRAPHY

Attention now focuses on an example of well-planned geographical learning in action. Two accounts set the scene for discussion. The first introduces the reader to an environmental studies day visits centre, where children are able to engage in a wide range of field study experiences. This account illuminates the centre's range and wealth of opportunities and potential for curriculum development in the areas of geography and environmental education. Following on from that is a description of classroom interpretations of first-hand experiences at the centre by one class of Key Stage 1 children. The topic pursued by this class is then summarised in a systematic way, which illustrates principles of planning and organisation used by the classroom teacher concerned.

The field centre: An introductory glimpse at the starting point for learning and investigation

The Environmental Studies Centre is an oasis of tranquillity in the bustling heart of England's second city, adjacent to one of the busiest main roads leading to Spaghetti Junction, and within walking distance of the city centre with its high-rise stores, hotels and offices, crowded pavements and ever-tangled traffic.

A long leafy driveway leads from the road into this haven of peace, winding through trees and bushes, gradually opening out to reveal magnificent gardens, an orchard, greenhouses, poultry pens, a pond, woodland and an exceedingly well-camouflaged single-storey classroom building.

The door of this building is open. Mrs Stanley stands at its entrance, ready to welcome a party of 6–7 year old visitors from their multi-ethnic, inner-city classroom. Like other classrooms, her building contains desks and chairs, but there the resemblance ends. As the children enter the room mouths open wide in astonishment. To many, it must seem as if they have stumbled upon an Aladdin's cave of treasures.

They gaze around a room brimming over with colourful and in some cases bizarre bric-à-brac like a botanical Steptoe's yard: squat inflatable vinyl frogs jostle for position with collage bees and honeycombs, globes, microscopes, soft toy animals, vegetables grown in the Centre's garden and the reconstructed skeleton of a young fox found in the grounds; large collages and embroidered hangings depicting many plants and animals, together with food chain mobiles, are suspended from the beams of the classroom roof, spinning gently in the breeze from the open door; the walls are covered with posters, sketches, paintings, maps, graphs and written work from various schools, while incubators, brooder boxes and lugubriously bubbling fish tanks bear witness to the presence of living creatures in this young naturalist's 'curiosity shop'.

This is obviously a room in which children do not merely sit passively, but are encouraged to be active – to observe, think and do, using their eyes, their ears and their imaginations. Although in some ways it is the focal point of the children's work during their half-day visits, in other ways the classroom is merely the meeting point from which to disperse and explore other aspects of the Field Centre.

Mrs Stanley takes them on a guided tour of the Field Centre and its five different habitats – the garden, the woodland, the pond, the field and the nature reserve. Some habitats are formally maintained, others are not. During this time, it is easy to see the curiosity and excitement of the children gradually increasing as they discover the rich, extensive resources of the Centre:

'Look miss, there's a wasps' nest!'
'I saw a fox's den – and some speckled wood butterflies.'

'There's lots growing in the garden – crab apples, pears, runner beans,
carrots, lettuce, onions, cereals, cabbages . . .'
'Ugh! I hate cabbage.'
'It is good for us, isn't it, miss?'
'Why?'

There are many other sights to see, surrounded as the children are by the
glory and variety of trees in the grounds, with oak, hawthorn, horse-chest-
nut, laurel, cherry, sycamore, guelder-rose, broom, yew, pine and beech,
among others. Fruits and seeds can be collected and discussed. Greenhouse,
bird box, beehive and weather station offer other opportunities for study.
In autumn, the ground is strewn with a quilt of leaves which can be
collected, identified and examined at the Centre, before being taken back
to school to form the basis of numerous other activities. As the children
gather armfuls of leaves, questions spring out like water from a fountain:

'I've got ten different sorts of leaves to take back, miss. How long do you
think it will take me to find out which trees they came from?'
'I like all the different shapes – I wonder how many of them are symmet-
rical?'
'What about all the colours? I'm going to make a list of all the different
shades I've seen. Then I can try to mix them all in paint.'
'How can we measure how high the trees are without climbing up them?'
'What's the biggest tree in the world, miss?'
'How do plants find food to keep them alive? Do they just live on
rainwater?'
'Are evergreens really always green?'

As autumn gives way to spring and spring in turn to summer, the school
continues to visit the Field Centre. The many flowers growing in the
grounds are identified and discussed. Seeds are collected and sown in pots;
soon words like 'germination' and 'pollination' will become almost second
nature to the children as they learn more about flowers, fruits and seeds.

'How do you think the seeds are spread, children?'
'The wind might blow them away, miss.'
'Some of them might get caught in an animal's coat, and get brushed off
again later.'
'Miss, I've got another idea – perhaps a bird might fly off with a seed in
its beak, and then drop it on the ground instead of eating it.'

The children are quick to notice and comment upon the wildlife sharing the
grounds of the Field Centre with them. The habitats are home to many
different creatures – from the strutting cockerel and his flock of hens,
amiably cohabiting with a paddling of ducks, to the foraging squirrels
rustling through the trees and the many species of bird life wheeling

overhead. Each creature has its own fascination for the human observers; some can be seen at close quarters, in the grounds or at the bird table, while others require binoculars to capture a fleeting glimpse of a flickering tail or a bright blinking eye. Even a cast-off feather is a source of wonder:

'It feels . . . like . . . greasy, sir.'
'Do birds get wet when it rains?'
'Are squirrels like rodents, miss?
'We've got some near us. They keep pinching all the food we leave out for the birds.'
'Look, there's a robin. I thought we only saw them at Christmas time.'
'I wonder how it got its red breast . . .'

At first glance, the pond seems unoccupied – apart from a pair of dabbling mallards who, having been disturbed, stare silent and disdainful at their visitors through the reeds. Closer inspection soon reveals a teeming mass of mini-beasts waiting to be scooped up and surveyed, collected and classified, respected and returned to the water.

'Hey, John – what's a pooter for?'
'Dunno. Pooting, I suppose.'

The children soon become absorbed in the search for these creatures, marvelling at the intricacy of their tiny bodies, the delicacy of their wings – and the number of their legs.

Back in the classroom, magnifying containers help the pond-dipping detectives in their task of separating insect from arachnid, mollusc from crustacean. Pencils hover and dart over paper, brows furrow in concentration as the children try to capture the catch a second time . . . sometimes a third and fourth.

Also housed in the classroom building are numerous other creatures – guinea pig, lizard, locust, rabbit, gerbil, Chinese hamster, leaf insect, salamander, snake, axolotl and pachnoda beetle, as well as an aviary of small birds and tanks of tropical fish. All grist to Mrs Stanley's mill.

'There's so much to see, miss. I think my brain will burst if I try to remember everything.'

Under Mrs Stanley's guidance, some of the children's questions may be answered at the Field Centre itself; others may deliberately be left for them to investigate back at school, while a few problems may never be neatly or completely solved. Options and approaches are left entirely to the interests and enthusiasms of the individual teacher. Each is free to delve into this rich seam of first-hand experiences. The process may be an intricate and complex one, but therein lies both the inspiration and the challenge.

St Wilfred's School and its year 2 class

Mrs Scott of St Wilfred's School has a warm personality and an enterprising approach to both the work and the children themselves. She is friendly, relaxed and softly spoken, harnessing all the skills of a good children's TV presenter. Her classroom has a friendly, rumpled, 'lived in' look, always packed with colour from books, posters, frieze boards and mobiles, and with evidence of a variety of written and practical activities scattered haphazardly around – a room for children rather than a classroom, where plimsolls, pipe cleaners and paint pots mingle carelessly with soft toys, string and scissors in a ragbag of cheerful chaos. The children themselves are seated in mixed-ability groups and actively encouraged to exchange ideas, question and help each other as much as possible.

Much of the autumn term was spent on an integrated topic entitled 'Food, Glorious Food'. The children had returned from their early visits to the Field Centre clutching a number of fruits and vegetables from the grounds to study, having also tasted a number of unusual food including lychee, olive and ginger. Back at school, Mrs Scott took each item of Field Centre produce in turn asking, 'Which parts do we eat?' Answers varied from item to item.

'The root, miss.'
'The stem.'
'The leaf, miss.'

Eventually, one of the children observed: 'It's not always the same, is it? Why not?'

Various theories were exchanged and the children spent some time investigating the problem. Afterwards these vegetables were classified, measured, sketched, painted, written about, depicted in cross-section and in collage form, and some were eventually cooked. Truly a case of 'read, learn and inwardly digest'! Climate and soil conditions necessary for their growth were investigated.

Throughout this process the children were constantly encouraged to use all their senses when handling the produce, to move freely around the room in search of books and apparatus, and to discuss these observations with their friends. From this beginning, the scope of the topic was widened to include numerous other aspects of food; a study of various tins and packets enabled the children to discover the main ingredients of our foods, as well as some basic ideas about nutrition and geographical origins of foods; one frieze board was fully occupied by a colourful cutaway diagram of the human digestive system, another was devoted to the rules of good food hygiene; and another contained a world map showing the origins of some of the foods available in our stores. Graphs of favourite snacks, fruits and dishes were drawn, based on statistics taken from all the classes in the school, and the children were encouraged to produce the 'mouthwatering-est' menu they could imagine.

> 'I'd start with melon, then I'd have roast beef and Yorkshire pudding, and I'd finish off with strawberries and cream.'
> 'What about fish fingers and ice cream?'
> 'Not on the same plate, John!'

It was pointed out that not all foods can grow in our own country, and reasons for this were discussed.

The latter activity was later extended to include the menu they would offer customers if they were running their own restaurant, and the menu card later became a useful exercise in handwriting practice. The menu itself stimulated some animated discussions, with much debate as personal tastes clashed with more commercial considerations.

> 'And I'd have lots and lots of chips . . .'
> 'You can't have chips with everything.'
> 'Why not?'
> "Cos not everybody's like you. If you're running a restaurant, you have to cater for what other people like. You need a choice of different things.'
> 'Why?'
> 'So people will come again. If people are going out to eat, they don't want something ordinary – you can get that at home. And chips are ordinary.'
> 'But lots of people buy chips every day – you can make plenty of money selling chips.'
> 'But not everybody likes chips.'
> 'I do. I'm always having chips.'
> 'Too much chips isn't good for you, is it, miss? You'll turn into a chip one day. Serve him right, wouldn't it, miss?'

Mrs Scott was not slow to respond.

> 'I wonder what might happen if David did turn into a chip one day. Let's write a story about it.'

Needless to say, a number of imaginative and curious scenarios about David's transformation were created, and read out to the rest of the class one Friday afternoon with great delight. Mrs Scott placed no restrictions upon the scope of the stories, with the result that many of them bordered on the surrealist. Throughout the writing of these and many other stories, Mrs Scott acted as a catalyst in sparking off the class imagination, fully prepared to take the risk of allowing the children to experiment with ideas and thus express their own personalities freely.

It was at this stage that the more epicurean members of the class expressed a desire to investigate some of today's more exotic 'foreign' foods – including spaghetti, curries, pizzas, snails and frogs' legs. This was a wonderful link with teaching about distant lands. Accounts of origins of these dishes were researched from library books and magazines in school, while parents and family friends were persuaded to send recipes and cookery tips. Perhaps the ultimate manifestation of parental involvement came with the organisation of a number of 'dinner parties' for the children to try out these recipes after school. Not only were the children learning theoretically in school, but they were also able to practise life skills outside it by being a host or a guest at these functions. Some children were even taken to 'a real restaurant' for the first time, as a direct result of the enthusiasm generated by their classroom work.

From the real thing, the children went on to design fantasy foods of their own – new ideas for breakfast cereals inspired a number of descriptions and paintings of unconventional flavours, colours, products and packaging. Once again, no restrictions were placed on the imaginations of the children, with the result that a remarkably wide range of expression soon became evident. Even the mixing of paint colours became a problem-solving exercise, as the children were encouraged to experience and to find out for themselves. Observing Nilesh, hunched over his paper and absorbed in the design of his latest market leader, Mrs Scott asked the class, 'Does anyone fancy a purple breakfast cereal?' The prospect was not universally popular. When he was asked what he intended to call it, back came Nilesh's answer: 'Beetawix, miss.' Francis spent some time perfecting various bizarre new flavours, including raw octopus and garlic flakes. 'It's for people who don't like breakfast,' he explained.

The study of food was later extended by reference to food supplies for people from farming, and those in the natural world, bringing in aspects of human geography and physical geography. Back at the Field Centre, the children were intrigued at the range of food needed by the ducks, hens and wild birds there. Various mobiles depicting different food chains were soon suspended from the classroom ceiling. A considerable amount of written work sprang from these researches, and the subject of food readily lent itself to song and story – *Charlie and the Chocolate Factory* and *James and the Giant Peach* being particular favourites. The Dahl tales inspired numerous pieces of writing about new confections and culinary adventures, which the children took great delight in reading to each other.

The extent to which the class as a unit constantly supported its individual members was quite remarkable, and sprang no doubt from the sense of a learning adventure being shared by everyone, including Mrs Scott. She was honest enough to admit when there were questions to which she did not know the answers, turning a potentially awkward situation to good account by involving the entire class in trying to discover solutions to problems.

Indeed, whenever the class was observed during the progress of this topic, the children were engaged in a variety of purposeful activities focused on geography, yet ranging from mathematics, science and language to drama, music, and art and craft work. Throughout the proceedings Mrs Scott remained discreetly in control, prompting and inspiring without dictating or dominating.

Following on from the initial starting point of food, the class studied bird life (and its food) at the Field Centre. A new sub-topic was under way in the classroom, clearly linked to and developing out of the main topic.

In addition to noticing and identifying the various species around the Centre, observing them through binoculars, representing the numbers pictorially, drawing and painting the birds, and finding out about their habits from posters and books, the children began to take account of the number of different species in and around the St Wilfred's School grounds. Birds of both fact and fantasy were painted and modelled in papier-mâché, frieze boards became aviaries and the classroom ceiling was festooned with colourful bird mobiles. Feathers from a variety of birds ranging from the sparrow to the lordly peacock were investigated under microscopes, arousing both curiosity and wonder: 'Look at the little hooks linking it together . . .' Simple experiments were carried out on these feathers to demonstrate how waterproof they were. One group of children set out to discover as many uses for feathers as they could, and eventually came up with ten different functions. Some children tried making wings from card, laying out the individual feathers so that they overlapped in the same way as a bird's primary and secondary feathers do. Others studied pictures of the bones in a bird's wing and compared them with the bones of a human hand and arm. Indeed, the topic gave rise to worksheets of various kinds but, perhaps unusually, these were skilfully employed as aids to learning rather than as the focus of the lesson.

The whole class was fascinated by the concept of bird migration, which as skilfully developed into a focus on mapwork. Nughman spoke for many:

'How do they know which way to go when they couldn't read a map if they had one?' (This prompted many activities relating to maps and map reading.)

The children often spent time discussing the workings of animal instinct, and deciding whether or not similar instincts existed in human beings.

'Humans are cleverer than animals, aren't they, miss?'
'Does that mean we can do everything better than they do, children?'
'Course we can. Our brains are bigger than theirs.'
'I don't think Dawn's right, miss. We can build flying machines, but we can't do it ourselves, can we?'
'We couldn't find our way for hundreds of miles without a map, miss.'
'I think animals and people are clever in different ways, miss. Like our class – we're all good at some things, but not always the same things. Tommy's good at football, but he can't draw as good as Jason.'

Another highlight of this topic work came when a group of interested children collected twigs and grasses from the neighbourhood of the school and tried to build birds' nests, using soil and water to make 'real mud'. The theory of human supremacy over the animal kingdom was severely tested, as the children soon began to realise that the task was not as easy as they had anticipated. Nevertheless, they persisted in their endeavours with untiring determination; even the child whom it was most difficult to motivate became absorbed in the nest-building activities and, when interrupted, was heard to remark to the offender: 'Shurrup, I'm doin' somethin' delicate!' As James, elbow-deep in muddy twigs after an hour's concentrated effort, and wrestling with a creation somewhat akin to a lopsided pincushion, wryly observed: 'This is the last time I call anybody birdbrain.'

Various other activities were incorporated into this topic on birds; the children heard legends and folk stories about birds from all over the world, and these again formed an excellent lead into work on distant lands. They wrote their own poems and stories about birds, and sang songs about them too. The children tried to imagine what life as a bird might be like. They did not find this easy – as Salma remarked, 'It's not easy writing in me when I'm trying to think in bird.' Thanks to the enthusiasm of the children and the inspiration of Mrs Scott the topic seemed to snowball, almost taking on a life of its own as time went by.

Not only did the class's knowledge of bird species improve but as their confidence and interest grew they became less inhibited in their approach to other lessons, seeming increasingly capable of solving (or attempting to solve) other problems in flexible and imaginative ways. A typical example came with the challenge to design a squirrel-proof bird table, which produced a number of ingenious Heath Robinson style drawings and explanations, involving the liberal use of baits, camouflage, trap doors, catapults, mallets and similar anti-squirrel devices. The end results successfully attracted further birds and increased motivation for the topic as a whole.

ANALYSIS

An analysis of this topic, brought to life in the account of classroom work, indicates that a number of the significant principles pertaining to good quality planning and organisation of work have been adhered to. As a whole, the topic covers a number of key curriculum areas, notably geography, science, mathematics, English and art. Geography is a discernible core, while cross-curricular links are meaningful. It does not attempt to include other foundation subjects that have no immediate or obvious connection for the sake of 'dragging them in'.

While the basic approach to planning and organisation is through a topic, teaching and learning include all the three approaches to organisation illuminated earlier in this chapter; namely, building upon children's first-hand experiences, integration of subject matter, and teaching subject-specific knowledge in its own right. A good example of the last of these approaches is the focus on mapwork skills which occurred when the sub-topic of migration arose.

Let us turn to planning details. The first stage of planning in the above example involved making a list of the projected content of the broad topic, showing subject areas with obvious links (Table 3.1). This and subsequent figures are in no way intended to be comprehensive, but serve to illustrate stages in the planning process which are transferable to any school situation.

Table 3.1 Food: geographical content and cross-curricular links

Broad topic content	Curriculum areas
What I like to eat – favourite foods – the importance of food	Geography, science, health education
Where our food comes from – where we buy it, where it grows	Geography, environmental education
Food stores in the local area – maps, types, distribution	Geography, mathematics
Who grows our food? – work of farmer. Types of farm	Geography, science, technology
Factors necessary for food production – weather, soil, etc.	Geography, science
Food chains – focus on bird life	Geography, science, art
Migration – search for food	Geography, science, mathematics

This was followed by a similar analysis of the key concepts and skills of the topic, teasing out those specific to geography (e.g. skills of graphicacy) and those which are essentially cross-curricular (e.g. numeracy, problem-solving). At this stage, opportunities for cross-curricular development of attitudes and values were also identified (e.g. inequality of food availability between nations, conservation of food supplies). This stage of analysis could well be recorded on a series of topic webs, with details of attainment targets added as the planning is 'firmed up'. Separate webs could be drawn, i.e. one for knowledge/content, one for concepts, one for skills, or this information could be combined into one comprehensive topic web, perhaps colour coded to separate knowledge, skills and concepts applicable to each subject area. Figure 3.1 illustrates how a web might be constructed in the first instance, before more detailed analysis of concepts, skills and attitudes is attempted. A combination of the presentation of ideas in the ways shown in Table 3.1 and Figure 3.1 provides a focus on content which should be helpful for teasing out the topic's discernible core of geography and its meaningful and sensible links with other curriculum areas.

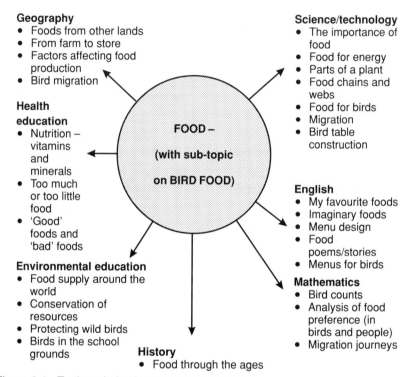

Geography
- Foods from other lands
- From farm to store
- Factors affecting food production
- Bird migration

Health education
- Nutrition – vitamins and minerals
- Too much or too little food
- 'Good' foods and 'bad' foods

Environmental education
- Food supply around the world
- Conservation of resources
- Protecting wild birds
- Birds in the school grounds

**FOOD –
(with sub-topic
on BIRD FOOD)**

Science/technology
- The importance of food
- Food for energy
- Parts of a plant
- Food chains and webs
- Food for birds
- Migration
- Bird table construction

English
- My favourite foods
- Imaginary foods
- Menu design
- Food poems/stories
- Menus for birds

Mathematics
- Bird counts
- Analysis of food preference (in birds and people)
- Migration journeys

History
- Food through the ages

Figure 3.1   Topic web: basic content and concepts

The final stage of general planning of this topic (before the specifics of lesson plans and learning tasks were considered) involved more detailed recording of the precise geographical content. For example:

Skills   Fieldwork techniques – observing food growing, observing birds, recording, identifying and classifying birds and food types.

Use of maps – plotting migration journeys, maps of the

local area showing food stores, practice in use of direction, scale and orientation.

Content   Food availability in local areas.

Role of soil and weather in food production. Reasons for bird migration.

Movement of food supplies – trade. Who sells? Who buys?

Food as a resource. Places where food cannot grow. Conservation. The significance of birds in the natural world.

From this level of detail, precise planning of lessons and learning tasks for groups and individuals could be done, taking account of levels of attainment and also allowing for that all-important degree of flexibility which goes hand in hand with active learning and field experiences. No geographical topic should be so rigorously planned that it has little scope for spontaneity deriving from children's 'on the spot' motivation, enthusiasm and excitement.

When a topic is planned around an issue or content area of environmental education, rather than geography *per se*, documentation will need to reflect this cross-curricular basis as well as the threefold nature of environmental education (for, in and about the environment). Geographical attainment targets will arise out of environmental starting points rather than as a baseline for incorporating them. A helpful model to be borne in mind when planning environmental topics might well be one that consists of two mutually dependent components. This can be expressed as a matrix in which the vertical component corresponds to the core and foundation subjects and the horizontal component corresponds to the cross-curricular theme of environmental education. Both components reflect the relevant range of knowledge, understanding and skills and will demonstrate a great deal of common ground. No doubt this model sounds rather abstract and complex. A simpler analysis of environmental topics, key issues involving knowledge and skills to be developed, is a useful place to start when building up a more complex planning model. Table 3.2 shows how this could be done, using the starting point of 'water'. From this simple table, a more elaborate analysis of skills and areas of knowledge and understanding can be derived, and further columns could be added to show the precise learning objectives and attitudes that it is planned to develop.

This schema will then form a basis for topic development and, most important, for linking a specific topic into a coherent and progressive overall curriculum plan for the key stage as a whole.

From practical examples, we now turn to the more general issues of planning topic work in geography. Organisation and planning should take account of a whole-school and class curriculum plan as well as details of

Table 3.2 Planning model: topics in environmental education/environmental geography

Topic	Education about the environment	Education for and in the environment	Links with ATs	Cross-curricular skills
Water	Water supply – and its problems	Visits to pond, river in locality, detailed observation of water life and quality	Geography ATs 1, 2, 3, 4 Science ATs 1, 2	Observation Numeracy
	Conservation of water	Identification of water plants and animals	Geography ATs Technology ATs 1, 2, 3, 4, 5	Problem-solving
	The hydrological cycle and effects of human activity on this	Weather studies – measuring rainwater	Geography ATs 1, 3, 5	Study Communication
	Salt and fresh water life	Simple experiments to measure pollution in water	Geography ATs 1, 2, 3, 5 Science ATs 1, 2, 4	Personal and social
	Water pollution (in both salt and fresh water environments)	Sub-topic on a distant environment – the oceans and investigation of threats to marine life	Geography ATs 1, 2, 3, 4, 5	

Notes: 1 The above is by no means comprehensive; it merely gives suggestions for each column.
2 English will be addressed throughout the topic.
3 ATs relate to the original National Curriculum Orders, which does not detract from the table as an example of a planning model.

individual topics, or other ways of approaching teaching in this area. School staff will need to discuss:

- how much time is to be allocated to geography-based topics/when they are to fit into the overall curriculum plan;
- whether the topic-work approach is to be supplemented by teaching specific skills or content of geography in their own right at any stage;
- the overall balance of links between geography-based topics and other areas of the curriculum – this can, of course, only be done in context when individual topics are designed;
- arrangements for assessment, record-keeping and evaluation of schemes/topics/the plan as a whole;
- availability of appropriate range of resources.

The school plan will need to cover the whole of the Key Stage and make provision for 'bridging' with Key Stage 2. It should bear in mind the agreed criteria for selecting places and themes to study, and the overall balance of attainment targets. There is scope for flexibility, as schools have freedom to make choices about places to be studied, how geographical work will be linked across the curriculum, and how the various elements of the programme of study will be combined into well-integrated topics or other subject-specific schemes. An important aspect of planning is a consideration of the interrelationships of two or more topics through time. Indeed, it is only through careful linking that the National Curriculum content will be covered coherently. *Non-Statutory Guidance* makes the key point that although topics need to have a distinct focus, links between them (and with other parts of the curriculum) can be made in a number of worthwhile ways:

- Topics can be linked to give a unifying theme to a year's work.
- Topics can be taught so that they draw on knowledge and understanding acquired in previous topics.
- The timing of a topic should take account of other parts of the curriculum.
- Topics should show how the attainment targets are related.

(NCC 1991)

Topics in year 1 (and indeed with reception children) could be centred around the children themselves and the locality, with personal life experiences being the unifying element (my family, my home, how I get to school, what I wear, what I eat, etc.). It seems an obvious point that topics should draw on knowledge and understanding of previous topics, yet it seems common practice in schools to leap in a rather haphazard way from one topic to another; 'water' to 'Easter', to 'change' to 'food' or whatever. In geography, perhaps more than in any other curriculum area, there is ample opportunity to build upon knowledge and skills acquired in topics relating to the local environment in a structured and progressive way, gradually moving onwards and 'outwards' into the study of distant and contrasting places. A simple progression from a topic on 'myself' to 'food/shopping' allows for the progressive introduction of content on distant lands through foreign food items and availability of foods. Topics should be organised like a jigsaw puzzle, so that they fit together, reinforce and elaborate upon previous learning, gradually building up the overall picture of geographical knowledge appropriate for the early years.

Opportunities for links with other areas of the curriculum will inevitably be more obvious and extensive in some themes than in others. Again, it is not enough to leave such links to chance. Careful planning should include decisions on such matters as whether, for example, scale should be introduced first in mathematics or in geography, at what stage, and in what topics it will be reinforced.

Geographical topics, and links between topics, should have and show a clear understanding of how the various elements of the content of geography are related. Several localities could be studied at any one time in order to cover physical, human and environmental geography, or one place may allow for successful integration of these elements, that is, the teasing out of the all-important links between them. It is by a gradual extension of content and the building-up of an increasing complexity of skills and understanding that learners will come to understand such links and progression in learning will be achieved.

Progression involves:

- gradual extension of content to include different places, environments, human activities and physical processes;
- increasing the scale of place studies from localities, regions and countries, to international and global;
- increasing complexity of the phenomena studied and tasks set;
- use of more generalised knowledge and abstract ideas;
- increasing precision required in practical and intellectual tasks;
- increasing awareness and understanding of social, political and environmental issues involving different attitudes and values.

(NCC 1991)

In practical terms, planning needs to take account of what and how best to teach so that learners are working towards the next level of attainment. One way of approaching this complex task is to group linked elements of content through a topic, and to specify the sequence in which they could be introduced in the topic. For example, this could mean that all children study a general topic on water, learning about it in its different forms and investigating what it looks like in the landscape, perhaps studying a pond or a river in the locality. They could then go on to investigate how weather affects water in the landscape (rainwater fills up ponds, causes rivers to flow faster, etc.) with opportunities for some learners to pay attention to different surfaces and slopes and how these affect rainwater when it reaches the ground. Elements of content have thus been grouped, e.g.:

1   Water and its functions in the environment;
2   Weather patterns and forms in which water occurs in the environment;
3   Physical effects of what happens when rainwater reaches the ground.

Such grouping allows for progression and takes account of relevant content. It also has a specific geographical context which can be linked to a progressive study of places, from the locality to distant environments. Furthermore, it assists in the processes of record-keeping and assessment which are, at least in part, about gathering evidence to monitor children's progress. If planning incorporates progression, the tasks of gathering and interpreting this evidence and monitoring progress are assisted. Observation of children at work, talking with them, questioning, listening and assessing materials produced by them will provide evidence of achievement which can be analysed in the context of the grouped elements of content.

Further details of whole-school policy and related aspects of record-keeping and assessment in geographical education are discussed in Chapter 5, after further case studies of good practice have been presented.

Chapter 4

Case studies of good practice

INTRODUCTION

This (substantial) chapter provides a number of case studies of good practice in geographical education and environmental geography in the first three years in school, gleaned from various schools and individuals.

The purpose of including these examples is to provide practical illumination of some of the theoretical issues highlighted and addressed throughout the book. The focus of the studies varies in terms of scope and range; some are at the level of whole-school matters, others focus on specific classroom topics and approaches to teaching and learning. Together they supplement and reinforce issues illustrated by way of practical examples elsewhere in this volume; for example, in Chapter 5 on assessment and record-keeping, and in Chapter 7 on resources.

INDEX OF CASE STUDIES

1 DEVELOPING AND USING THE SCHOOL GROUNDS IN THE EARLY YEARS

Summary of project

This school grounds development project was engaged in with children across the primary age range. Some background material is provided, followed by examples of work undertaken with the youngest children in the school.

The conservation area was started with the help of Wigan Groundwork Trust. The children worked alongside adults, helping with the digging and planting of the site. The children had discussed and planned what they wanted in the area. Plans were drawn up, the necessary permission given and the work went ahead. Initially the site consisted of a pond and a rocky area for wildlife shelter. This was surrounded by a path consisting of circular wooden blocks to make an attractive feature and create crevices for insects. The path was continued with woodchip and stepping stones. To the front of this was an area of scree. The surrounding grass at this time was mainly tough rye grass.

Unfortunately the pond was vandalised and all the large rocks were thrown into the water, damaging the liner. It was rebuilt and a marshy edge was added at one side to encourage more pond life. The children were able to do some pond dipping and they incubated eggs in a related topic. The ducklings that were hatched enjoyed a good swim on the pond. Yet once again the area was vandalised and once more needed repairing. This time we measured the depth of the pond and dug out a series of shelves. We built a wall of stones and soil and encased it in thick mud. We used stones so that if it was jumped on it would remain solid. The smaller hollow behind the wall was to be the marsh or bog garden. The older children took measurements and did calculations to make certain that the overflow would go into the marsh area. It was a great success, though expensive as we had to buy another liner – even though we also reused the existing one.

The pond was finished and looked lovely on the Friday. By Monday it was ruined and our wooden path dug up and thrown into it. However, during this time we had also been removing the turf from an area around the pond to create a mini-meadow. The turf was used to construct a small hill and was placed on top of all the rocks and stones that had been thrown in the pond. The children worked very hard. In this hill we also made lizard tunnels. The seed was sown for the meadow in early autumn and has been quite successful. To one side of the meadow we planted a lavender and southernwood hedge.

Two butterfly gardens were also constructed within the area and one in the nursery playground which runs alongside the conservation area. We also planted nettles, honesty and nasturtiums to attract caterpillars. While excavating these sites the children made habitat piles of stones under the denser rose bushes to act as invertebrate habitats. We have also constructed habitat piles of twigs, cut grass and leaves.

The children have planted acorns around the edge of the garden and holly, hawthorn and buddleia to create a mixed hedge. As yet this is very young.

The children made bird boxes, bat boxes and a bird table to enhance the conservation area.

Figure 4.1 provides a diagrammatic representation of the development.

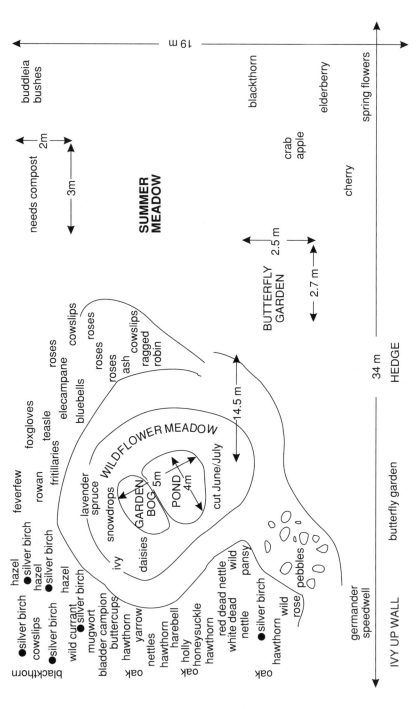

Figure 4.1 The school grounds development project

Future plans

One of the reasons for including this case study is to show how a school has coped with incessant vandalism – sadly a problem for many schools, particularly in inner-city areas. Because of this, more thought is being given to pond design, in order to make the area 'less inviting'. Consequently it has been decided to create a marsh area in the existing pond site and to make small areas of water using clay as the base. As far as hedging is concerned, it is hoped:

- to extend the hedged area around the whole field site;
- to create an orchard of native trees in the lower corner of the field;
- to start a tree nursery;
- to create a cornfield meadow.

Early years curriculum work

A wide range of practical, investigatory activities derived from children's first-hand experiences in their school grounds development project. Figure 4.2 provides a topic web outline for activities centred on the pond as a feature. Similar planning focused on other elements of study.

As stated, a key issue addressed throughout this study was vandalism, and so further commentary intends to show how the teachers skilfully used this as a basis for discussion and reflection, thereby encouraging the development of awareness and concern for the environment in the children. What could have been seen as a negative feature of the school's development plans was used for extremely positive educational purposes. The children speak for themselves to illustrate this.

Why we created the garden

Rachel, aged 3

Nice flowers for the butterflies.

Darryl, aged 4

Planting flowers for the butterflies.

Geography links with science

Louise, aged 3

Those flowers are growing and the water is already in them and that is the soil. We are planting them for the butterflies.

Rebecca, aged 3

The rain in the soil when it is sunny will make them grow.

Christopher, aged 4

The flowers are growing in the muck but there is some water in it to make the flowers grow and it makes them [the roots] sink down and the flowers grow again.

Luke, aged 3

The seeds are ready to grow, we have put them inside a greenhouse made of plastic lids, we put them in the sunshine to grow.

Rachel, aged 3

We were planting seeds we put them in dirt then we gave them water then we put them in the sun to keep them warm.

Craig, aged 3

When the seed is growing massive plants will come out and the butterflies will eat them.

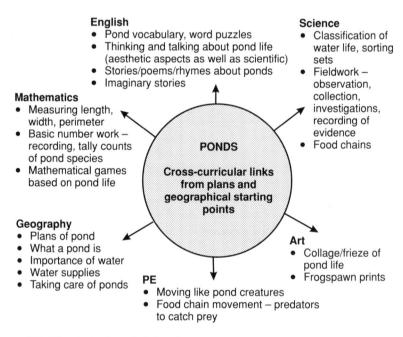

English
- Pond vocabulary, word puzzles
- Thinking and talking about pond life (aesthetic aspects as well as scientific)
- Stories/poems/rhymes about ponds
- Imaginary stories

Science
- Classification of water life, sorting sets
- Fieldwork – observation, collection, investigations, recording of evidence
- Food chains

Mathematics
- Measuring length, width, perimeter
- Basic number work – recording, tally counts of pond species
- Mathematical games based on pond life

Geography
- Plans of pond
- What a pond is
- Importance of water
- Water supplies
- Taking care of ponds

PONDS

Cross-curricular links from plans and geographical starting points

Art
- Collage/frieze of pond life
- Frogspawn prints

PE
- Moving like pond creatures
- Food chain movement – predators to catch prey

Figure 4.2   Ponds: topic web for project

Observations, action, concern

Jade, aged 4

> We are sad because they have spoiled our pond again. Thrown it all in and the frogs and beetles and fish will be dead now.

Christian, aged 4

> We will mend it again.

Luke, aged 4

> They have spoiled it, thrown stones in. We will mend it.

Laura, aged 4

> They have ripped the lining and pushed it down, all the water has gone in. The fish will have nowhere to live.

Ideas – how to stop people spoiling our pond

1 Put a fence around it – big.
2 Put a cage over it . . .
3 Put some wood round.
4 Put a wall round – glass.
5 Sign – Danger – Beware of the guard dog.

and from Jade (aged 4) Smack their bums.
      Laura (aged 4) Write a letter to the police.

As a result of such discussions and the involvement of the young learners, they were helped to develop a sense of ownership of their site and responsibility for it – a successful example of environmental geography in action.

Quite apart from educational gains in curriculum terms, a noticeable effect upon the children's behaviour was observed, illustrating a point made in the DES publication on discipline in schools:

> where pupils are provided with a pleasant environment they respect it, and where they have contributed to it, they treat it as their own . . . we believe this sense of participating in the ownership of a school plays an important part in the way pupils behave.
>
> (DES/Welsh Office 1989)

The project therefore contributed to the all-round social and personal education of the children through activities based on their immediate surroundings.

This case study therefore demonstrates how the youngest children in school can be encouraged to be reflective about environmental quality and personal action in the world; and can be helped to develop a sense of concern for their surroundings.

2   A TOPIC ON MAPWORK: DEVELOPMENT OF THE CONCEPT OF SPACE

This topic focuses on inclusion of geographical skills in the curriculum. Every Key Stage 1 child, no matter how young, can be introduced to one or more of the skills of mapwork. Planning for teaching in this area should take account of the basic elements of mapwork (Catling 1988) which provide the skills-based content for any scheme or topic. These are:

1   *Perspective* – presents features in plan form, enables us to see what is hidden from view at ground level.
2   *Position and orientation* – maps show how various features are related to one another in 'space' and where they are located. From them we can give directions. Systems of grid referencing enable us to give accurate locations.
3   *Scale* – maps are scaled-down versions of the real thing. A plan view of a landscape or place is represented on a piece of paper.
4   *Map content* – content varies from map to map. Some emphasise specific features, e.g. streets, buildings, height of land. Content is dependent on the purpose for which the map is intended and, of course, its scale.
5   *Symbols* – are used to indicate what is recorded in the map's content. A key is a related feature, necessary so that the map reader can interpret the symbols.
6   *Additional information* (maps often provide useful information to supplement the content symbols: e.g. names of streets, buildings, towns, etc., types of farmland, shops, age of historic sites).

This content serves to help meet the basic aim of the topic expressed in conceptual terms which is to develop the children's concepts of space and place, both fundamental to geographical education. The content should also be interpreted within the context of the National Curriculum requirements, concerned with skills.

A detailed topic plan can therefore be devised which includes reference to the specific geographical education which forms its central core, expressed in terms of content, concepts and skills, cross-referenced with the relevant attainment targets. It is then appropriate to consider which other areas of the curriculum will be addressed in implementing this plan so that meaningful links are identified and included in planning documentation.

The basic objectives of a mapwork topic may be to help children develop the following ideas (stated at the level of adult understanding):

- Maps and plans can be 'read' by understanding basic elements, e.g. symbols, scale, direction.
- Maps and plans tell us about places. They help to locate objects and places in relation to each other.
- Printed maps help to develop our 'mental maps' or images of the world.
- Maps suggest distinct territories in our modern world. Many geographical or environmental issues and concerns do not fall within neat and distinct national boundaries.

Theoretical background

Perhaps *formal* mapwork as such is not relevant to children who have recently entered school. Nevertheless, spontaneous mapping is definitely to be encouraged. These early maps are likely to be pictorial and egocentric. As demonstrated by Piaget and others (Piaget and Inhelder 1956, Piaget 1960b), by the age of about 4, children are beginning to understand the locations of objects which surround them in relation to one another, or in a topological sense. Topological cognitive maps (Catling 1978) will be drawn, which contain pictures (e.g. of home, school, trees, church) linked together in some way without the formality of orientation and scale. Such picture maps gradually acquire formality in the sense that connections will be made between objects. For example, a road may be drawn, perhaps in plan form, linking buildings that are still drawn pictorially. There will still be no accuracy of direction, orientation and scale. It is generally believed (Boardman 1983) that by the age of 7 children reach a stage of development in which a 'projective' representation of objects evolves from the topological. Such things as three-dimensional objects, e.g. buildings, will now be represented two dimensionally. A child of this age could well be producing that which more closely resembles a 'map' as we know it, with attention to detail, direction, orientation and scale, although these will be far from accurate in most cases.

Stages in the development of cognitive mapping may be summarised as follows:

A. *Topological (egocentric) stage.* Around 5 years of age. Children will draw 'link-picture' maps. Known places (drawn as pictures) will be connected in some way. Direction, scale, orientation and distance are non-existent.
B. *Euclidean (abstract) stage.* Around 10 years of age. Children will draw accurate and detailed maps which demonstrate abstract co-ordination. Scale, direction and symbolic representation will be well developed.

The quasi-egocentric and quasi-projective stages occur between these two. Children will gradually represent their localities and other places as quasi-maps, with increasing attention to detail and continuity of routes. They will show increasing ability to take account of direction, orientation, distance, scale and representation in plan form.

Clearly the first three years in school are the crucial period when pupils should be helped in their transition from topological to Euclidean operations.

A wide range of classroom tasks will assist in this progression towards formality and accuracy. Children can be encouraged to draw pictorial, spontaneous maps of such things as 'my house and street', 'my route to school', 'where I go to the shops'. Imaginative picture mapping can also arise from story time – many stories lend themselves to the illustration of journeys or to the reconstruction of places, as discussed in much greater detail in a later case study. This is an excellent cross-curricular link with English through story, discussion and vocabulary.

A key conclusion from research evidence on this topic is that no child in school is too young to be introduced to the appreciation and use of maps. Blades and Spencer (1986) tested the feasibility of teaching nursery age children about map use. Their research involved investigating whether children of this age could be taught how to orientate maps – an essential part of efficient map use. Results indicated that children who had received training in orientation both learned and remembered related skills. Conversely, it was found that a control group was unable to use maps efficiently, performing no better than if its members had been guessing.

Related experiments show that children quickly learn strategies for overcoming problems such as incorrectly orientated maps. This and other research evidence suggest that teachers should introduce mapwork to children much earlier than the traditional age of 7–8 years.

It should also be recognised that there is still much research to be done on the abilities required to use maps successfully, and on the development of mapwork skills. The complex mental abilities involved remain unclear. Consequently, there is no strong agreement on the best way of introducing maps to young children, or on the sequencing of mapwork skills. A range of ways of introducing early mapwork into the classroom has been suggested by writers in this field, and they include the use of plan views and aerial photographs. One common area of agreement deriving from research evidence is that geographical concepts are best learned within a particular context. Therefore, the most valuable mapwork activities will probably be those which are meaningful or real to the young learners.

Some of the activities which follow suggest a context (e.g. everyday objects in the classroom, the school playground). Others are presented in more abstract form in the hope that readers will adapt them for use in their own individual situations within the constraints of available resources.

Suggested activities

- Draw plans of everyday objects and use as the basis for comparing plan view with oblique view. Let the children draw around familiar objects on a piece of paper, e.g. key, eraser, pencil, stamp, building brick. Ask them to write a list of the things that remain the same about these objects (size, shape) and things that have changed (details of colour, patterning, texture). Introduce the key idea that plans represent three-dimensional objects in two dimensions. They are the bird's eye view or what we see from above.
- Extend the above activity by dividing children into pairs. One of each pair should provide plan drawings of six objects; the other has to guess which objects have been drawn around. Who can guess the greatest number accurately without needing clues? If necessary, children can provide clues by colouring their objects, adding patterns, details, etc. This underpins a basic understanding of the need to read and interpret plans and maps and the use of keys. It also (without consciously referring to the fact) limits plans at this stage to objects which will fit on to a piece of paper. The logical progression will be to introduce further activities requiring the use of scale.

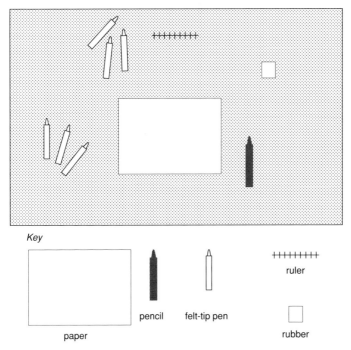

Figure 4.3 **My desk**

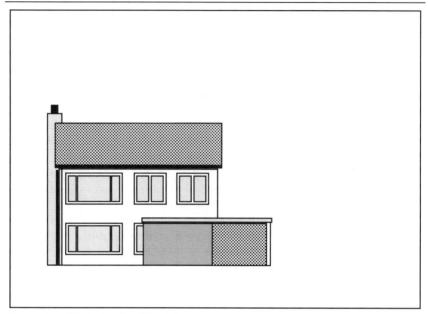

Figure 4.4   Worksheet outline (a)

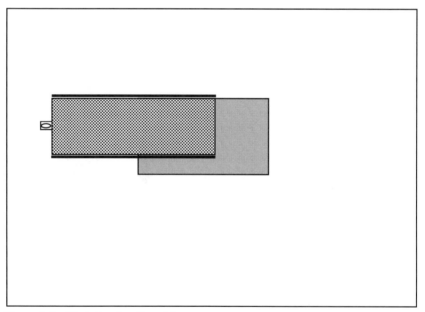

Figure 4.5   Worksheet outline (b)

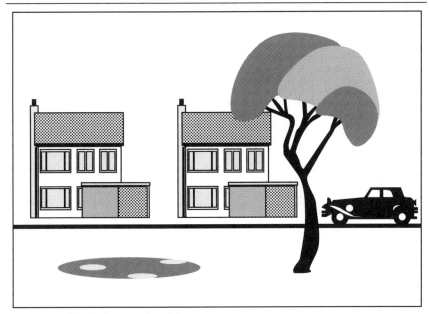

Figure 4.6   Worksheet outline (c)

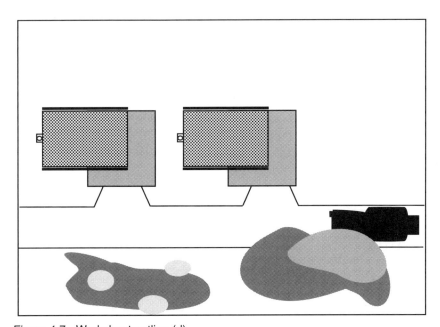

Figure 4.7   Worksheet outline (d)

- Let the children draw (without accuracy of scale at this stage) plans of other familiar, simple objects for their partners to interpret – perhaps plans of their desk (Figure 4.3). Incorporate keys after partners have made a 'good guess' without them.
- Discuss the key idea that, once plans are drawn, objects are 'fixed' on the paper in relation to each other. If the objects on the desk are rearranged, a new plan must be drawn to represent its accuracy. Stress that this is an important aspect of plans – they show us the fixed location of objects in relation to each other. Larger plans, for example, of rooms, streets and buildings, can therefore help us to find our way from 'object to object'. Explain that we usually use the word 'map' to describe the bird's eye view of larger areas, but maps have similar features to plans and serve the same purpose.

  At the simplest level, draw one object in oblique view, e.g. a house (Figure 4.4) and discuss what this would look like when drawn in plan form (Figure 4.5). Ask children to say what a bird would see when flying over it. Would it see the windows? There is endless scope for elaboration of this activity – as scenes become more complex (Figures 4.6 and 4.7).
- Many scenes of increasing complexity could be drawn for the children to 'match' and colour, and they could be asked to construct their own plans from the oblique view. Activities of this kind lead very well into discussion on the use of keys. Objects drawn can be colour coded to show an understanding of what matches with what in the two scenes. Boxes can be drawn below the diagrams to be coloured in as a key. This aspect of work also links with the development of skills of symbolic representation. As already mentioned, young children's natural inclination is to draw pictures rather than symbols. The drawing of plans from oblique views encourages discussion about suitable ways of representing the bird's eye view of objects ranging from everyday classroom items to the wider world of buildings, trees, railway lines, etc.
- Make 'object-in-plan-form' workcards for the children to interpret. Ask them to:
  1 Write down what the plan shows.
  2 Draw a picture of each object.
  3 Write down what aspects of the picture are hidden by the plan.
- Devise games so that the children draw around objects for their friends to try to identify – they can be coloured in and details added to make the drawings look like the real thing. Progress by asking children to imagine that a spider has walked on to their sheet of paper and wants to investigate all the objects depicted. Draw a path that the spider takes to visit all the objects. As the drawings are joined in this way, they are linked together in space and in the children's minds. This is an important mapwork concept. Activities like these can extend over several lessons, familiarising children with the idea that a map is a representation of

space occupied by objects depicted in plan form, and that the objects are in a fixed location in space.

- As a progression from such activities, children can be asked to construct their own maps (without accurate scale) and devise their own symbols. An important question can then be asked: How do other people interpret your symbols? Again, this links to an understanding of the need for a key, and the idea that many published maps have an agreed pattern of symbols that can easily be recognised. Ideas such as these link skills of map construction with the equally important skills of map reading and interpretation.

- Discuss the use of appropriate symbols for map interpretation. Ask the class to suggest why an agreed set of symbols is useful. What difficulties would arise if everyone's village plan had a different key? Let the children look at a range of similar scale Ordnance Survey maps. While they may not comprehend these in detail, they should be able to appreciate their common key. Point out certain universally agreed symbols, e.g. for rivers, footpaths, phone boxes.

- Take a polaroid camera out into the street. Photograph the view from various angles. Back in the classroom, analyse the content of the photographs. Let the children attempt to draw plans of the same scenes. Consider:
  – What appears on the photographs that could not be on a plan (e.g. children playing, traffic).
  – What can be shown on a plan that is not revealed by the photographs (e.g. what is behind shops and houses).

- If possible, obtain an aerial photograph of your locality. Compare this with a printed map. Let the children see how many features of the photograph they can identify on the map. What does the map not show?

- Consider the idea of scale. Children in the early years in school are surrounded by experience of this without conscious realisation or discussion of the fact. Use frequent opportunities to raise awareness of scaled-down versions of reality. Questions such as 'Why is the play house in the classroom smaller than a real house?' and 'Why is the dolls' cutlery smaller than that which we use at lunchtime?' will promote valuable geographical discussion, linked to the general development of vocabulary and conversation about everyday things. Introduce the formality of scale by asking how we could represent an object which is bigger than the piece of paper we want to draw it on. (This will lead on naturally from the 'drawing around familiar objects' activities already described as inevitably some children will have selected items that were bigger than their paper.) Initially, concentrate on a scale of half size, done best with pieces of paper or card in the first instance, and then (probably in year 2) progress to more complex scales and ideas on how we draw such things as our desk, the classroom, the school, the playground. While little formal work can be done in interpreting scales, do introduce children to a variety of published maps, partly as an awareness-raising exercise. They will see that not all maps are of the same scale; we have 'large scale maps' and 'small scale maps'; some maps show the whole world on a piece of paper, others show only the streets of the locality.

- Give practice in locating objects in relation to each other. Plenty of practice can be given in putting models back in the correct place, making sure that apparatus is placed in its correct order, etc. Perhaps a model village could be set out, and then reassembled so buildings and trees are replaced in similar positions. This is sound early years geography, affording practice in recording locations and in simple plan/map construction. Key vocabulary to be introduced includes 'opposite', 'in front of', 'by the side of', 'behind', 'next to'. The progression of these skills in later years will involve an understanding of grids and co-ordinates in order to make specific locations explicit. Such skills are linked to an understanding of direction, which in the early years involves familiarity with the vocabulary of 'right', 'left', 'backwards', 'forwards', etc., and an awareness of rotation of the self in space. Before formal points of the compass are introduced, give plenty of practice in turning through 90 degrees, 180 degrees, 270 degrees and 360 degrees, using terminology of turning to the right or left for a quarter-turn, half-turn, three-quarter turn and a whole turn. Formal elements of direction, the points of the compass, could be introduced at an appropriate stage, beginning with the four cardinal points – north, south, east and west.
- Help children to transfer the skills of understanding of direction to reading published maps. Consult a globe. Explain that north is the direction towards the North Pole from any other location. South is the direction towards the South Pole. East and west can be related to the rising and setting of the sun. If the time of year is appropriate encourage the children to observe the sunrise and sunset, noting thereby which rooms in their home face east and which west. Study published maps and note how direction is indicated.
- Much scope exists for linking PE activities with understanding of direction. Divide children into groups in the school hall or playground and play games where they are asked to follow instructions relating to movement through 90-degree angles. Five children in a group provide an ideal number, one in the centre and four at the cardinal compass points. Children can take it in turns to be in the centre and make appropriate movements. After each turn, the centre child must state who he or she is facing, who is behind, who is to the right and who to the left, thus reinforcing related vocabulary.

A final element of mapwork, that of relief, or height of land, is perhaps the most difficult of all to introduce at a formal level. How difficult it is even for adults to appreciate the abstract idea that a certain place is so many metres above the level of the sea and represented by contour lines. In the infant school, it is perfectly appropriate to reinforce basic vocabulary of relief, such as 'high up', 'low', 'hills', 'steep' and 'gentle', and to show maps which indicate that some land is higher than others. The relief of the locality can be discussed; perhaps some children have to walk up or down hills to get to school or to the shops, and some may visit hilly or mountainous areas, which can be described in terms of their being 'high up', with views 'over' other land which is 'lower'.

The above activities are specific to the development of understanding of the basic elements of mapwork. While pursuing these, have a good range of maps on display for children to observe. Even if the formality is beyond their conceptual capacity, young children will gain a great deal from awareness that various forms of map exist. It is perfectly appropriate to display as many forms of map-style representation as possible, including maps of the world, large-scale maps of the locality and school environment, street plans of your town or village, A–Z type maps and Ordnance Survey maps. Add to these regular displays of the children's own maps and maps of imaginary places.

This topic can be augmented by some valuable and more general cross-curricular interpretations of the theme. For example:

- Explore the origins of map-making. Thousands of years ago the very first 'maps' were mere scratches in soil or sand. Prehistoric people used symbols of this kind to help them find food, water and their way back home from a hunting expedition. Draw pictures of cave people carving a sign for water in the earth.
- Ask the children to make a list or talk about the variety of information we can obtain from world maps, e.g. locations of countries, oceans, names of major cities, rivers. Look at a variety of maps of one country (an ideal opportunity to demonstrate the use of atlases) and point out that maps can be devised to provide a wide range of information.
- Tell the story of Christopher Columbus, who sailed west in 1492 in search of the Indian Spice Islands. His famous voyage led to the discovery of two previously unmapped continents – North America and South America. Thus the world was seen by mapmakers to be a very different place.
- Read stories that tell of journeys across land and sea, both real and imaginary. Let the children draw spontaneous maps of fictional journeys and trace the route of factual ones on printed maps.

This case study on developing mapwork skills has been included for two reasons. First, to give a number of practical ideas which will be of use to anyone planning topics on this subject. Second, to demonstrate that mapping is an example of education which is specifically geographical, and therefore needs to be addressed in its own right as a discernible and critical area of learning; it can be linked in a meaningful way to other areas of the curriculum. Furthermore, to a large extent, it arises spontaneously out of traditional good practice in the early years classroom. It is an excellent example of how the skills of geography (in this case graphicacy) can contribute to the general intellectual development of children in the first three years in school.

3 BEYOND THE LOCALITY: TEACHING ABOUT DISTANT LANDS

The topic: invertebrates

This geographical topic on invertebrates from exotic, faraway places followed on from a previous scientifically focused topic on mini-beasts found in the school grounds. It was conducted with a mixed-ability year 2 class for half a term. It should be noted, however, that the invertebrates used, being natives of other countries, were acquired for the purpose of this topic and it was accepted that they became 'long-term' residents of the classroom. They could hardly be returned to the wild at the termination of the work in hand. This clearly was no disadvantage, as the children gained a great deal in terms of learning how to take care of these fascinating forms of life. Practical details of culture and rearing of suitable species are included at the end of the discussion of this topic, for the benefit of those readers wishing to pursue this theme. The emphasis which follows is on discussion of the topic and its appropriateness in terms of addressing some of the key issues relating to distant lands teaching, rather than on a lengthy description of practical classroom tasks.

As a whole, the topic forms a superb example of worthwhile geographical education linked with the core area of science. From the geographical perspective, a major aim was to help the children develop a sense of 'place', that essential element of geographical education concerned with the reciprocal relationship between people and their environment. This was achieved through the development of activities, as described below, which were based on real objects from distance places, thus creating the all-important concrete link between the learners and environments of which they had no personal experience. Emphasis throughout was on first-hand, investigatory tasks. Motivation for the topic was no challenge for the teacher concerned. The young learners were totally captivated by the fascinating appearance and, indeed, the sheer size of the creatures in question. One of the earliest questions to be investigated as giant hissing cockroaches, giant African land snails and giant millepedes ambled their way across squared paper, was how their sizes compared to the UK relatives of these species. Discussion and imaginative writing generated a wide range of relevant vocabulary, creative thinking and spontaneous suggestions for further investigations. Detailed observation paralleled measuring, experimentation, illustration and recording tasks. Movement, feeding, breathing, reproduction, life cycles and habits were observed, investigated and recorded in appropriate ways, covering a wide range of scientific, mathematical and cross-curricular skills (including observation, problem-solving and communication). From the immediate and the observable, the teaching skilfully steered questioning and investigation into the area of the native background of these creatures.

'Why don't we have millepedes this size in our country?'
'In which countries would you find such creatures in the wild?'
'What do they eat? . . . where do they live?'
'What is the weather like in their native lands?'
'Do they live in forests, or open lands?', etc.

Many questions were generated by the children as were answers, some of which were far more accurate than others. Gradually the topic evolved into twin sub-themes of 'Invertebrates of the Tropical Forest' and 'Invertebrates of the Desert'. A rather exciting and successful series of lessons ensued in which geographical/environmental knowledge and understanding emerged as a discernible and worthwhile core. Planning and organisation ensured that this focus covered a range of specific issues, incorporating knowledge, understanding and skills from the curriculum areas of both geography and environmental education.

Key attainment targets (of the original Order) covered in geography were AT2, Knowledge and Understanding of Places, and AT5, Environmental Geography, though all attainment targets were covered to some extent through the use of maps (AT1), investigations into weather and the invertebrates themselves (AT3), and human population and activities of forests and deserts (AT4). Content ranged across all the seven 'topics' of environmental education and incorporated a great deal of learning about forest and desert environments, and indeed *for* them. Issues of conservation were at the forefront of discussion. Young as these learners were, they demonstrated genuine concern for the need to preserve the world's timber resources and appreciation of the different ways of life of rain forest communities, and the problems of desertification and living in an arid zone.

Discussion

This topic illuminates many of the theoretical points and issues raised in Chapter 1. Research into children's knowledge, and awareness of distant lands in the early years reported there, showed that children have a range of basic understandings, alongside inevitable gaps in or erroneous knowledge, and perhaps biased or stereotypical knowledge. The teacher in this case study appreciated at the outset the need to find out as much as possible about the children's existing background knowledge of the distant lands which were to be studied, so that this could be built upon and indeed challenged constructively. She was aware of the children's incidental contact with places throughout the world, as a result of media contact, holidays, stories and personal contacts, and talked with them extensively about their ideas of forest and desert lands. She attempted to find out about the resultant 'mental maps' or images of these places held in the children's minds; the perhaps blurred 'world inside their heads'. She was also well aware of the issues of stereotyping and bias, and took positive steps to ensure that accurate, up-to-date images of rain forests and desert communities were presented to the class, bearing in mind the suggestion (Tajfel and Jahoda 1966) that children absorb, from the media and social discourse, attitudes and prejudices about other nations and peoples well before they learn accurate factual information about them. Furthermore, information available to the young child will be selectively sought, received and remembered, in ways that are supportive of pre-existing (pre-judged) categories (Tajfel 1981).

This approach took account of *Geography: Non-Statutory Guidance* (1991) which suggests that, when teaching about distant places, teachers should avoid possible pitfalls such as:

- portraying an outdated or stereotyped image of places and people (for example, modern life for the Inuit, as they prefer to be called, may involve working for the oil industry and living in houses rather than hunting and living in temporary shelters such as igloos);
- giving a limited view of a country (for example, that Sri Lanka only produces tea);
- using biased material about a country (for example, material which portrays only the attractions of living, working, or travelling in a country).

(NCC 1991)

Another key issue accepted by this teacher was the need to relate distant lands learning to reference points in the children's own lives. If tasks are in some way linked to the pupils' own locality or personal experiences, first, they will identify far more easily with the topic, place or people under consideration, and, second, they will be helped to develop an understanding of the interdependence of the modern world. Relevance may also help in the elimination of bias and stereotyping. If learners can feel a part of the 'total world' and appreciate the importance of links between nations, they may be less likely to view distant people as alien or remote from present-day reality and world issues. The distant lands dimension developed out of suitable reference points in the children's own lives, in this case, invertebrate animals which could be compared with their native counterparts.

To consider this point in general, there can be no better starting point than that which is 'real' and exciting to young children. Animals, plants, food, weather and homes are perhaps five of the most highly motivating and worthwhile connections between nations of the world which can be developed. The first three at least provide tremendous scope for using real objects as the point of contact between the children and the land of their origin. One single object, e.g. the snail, rubber plant or pineapple, could stimulate considerable motivation and generate a complete sub-topic on its natural environment. Alternatively, a collection of artefacts/souvenirs, maps, photographs, etc., could be established about the land to be studied.

A final, general issue to be picked up at this point concerns how decisions are made in a school about which places in the world are to be studied. The teacher in the case study described here focused upon two global environments – tropical rain forests and desert lands – and thus the approach was from a 'habitat' point of view rather than from the selection of one specific foreign town, state or country to study. Her decision was guided by the invertebrates available; in other words, the focus of the study or the links with the children's own lives dictated the areas of the globe that came under close scrutiny. That was a perfectly reasonable and acceptable method of selecting places. There are, however, other approaches to this task, and so a number of general points will be made.

Selection of places cannot be divorced from a more general discussion on planning the curriculum, so that a good range of places are studied across the Key Stage 1 (with appropriate 'bridges' into Key Stage 2). It is perhaps sensible to select places which:

- provide a balanced spread of knowledge of places around the world;
- cover a range of scales – local, regional, national and international;
- provide opportunities for adequate coverage of elements of content.

It seems sensible for schools, when working out curriculum plans and topics, to make a list of criteria for selection of places so that a balance is achieved. Such criteria might well include:

- Study of places of which teachers have personal experience. Thus they can talk knowledgeably about distant lands, having travelled there, lived and eaten there, viewed the scenery and talked with indigenous people. Objects, souvenirs and photographs in a personal collection will be valuable teaching aids.
- Study of places of which the children, their parents and friends have personal experience. Once again, souvenirs and photographs will be readily available, as will stories of 'real life' in the land. A class is far more

likely to be motivated by the study of somewhere that one of its members can speak of than somewhere selected at random.

- Study of places where school contacts and links can be developed. It would be extremely useful if, for example, the children could exchange letters, photographs, writing, weather statistics and news stories with children who live in the distant place. Contacts could be made in both foreign and distant UK locations. A school in London, for example, could 'twin' with one in the highlands of Scotland. An ongoing school link will be much more productive than a short-term exchange set up for the duration of a single topic.
- Study of 'topical' places – that is, ones which are receiving plenty of media coverage that can be a source of information, cuttings, photographs and discussion. Such places range from those enduring disasters to those hosting current events, e.g. the Olympic Games.
- Study of places from which interesting objects, plants or animals are available, this being the criterion used by the school referred to in the case study topic.

By implementing the above suggested set of valid criteria for selection of places to study, it is likely that a good range will be achieved, and that there will be a balance between places studied by the school regularly (with a wide range of resources built up for the purpose) and those studied on a one-off basis for some good reason. Whatever criteria are used, it should be emphasised that teaching and learning must aim to help children identify with the place or 'foreign' people under consideration. If they can feel a part of this world, and have a developing understanding of the interdependence of modern nations and societies, they may be less likely to view distant lands as totally alien, exotic or remote from their own reality.

Practicalities: some invertebrates from distant lands suitable for classroom rearing

Australian stick insects

This is a far larger and more spectacular insect than the more common Indian stick. The female is in fact one of the largest insects to be found in the world. There is a distinct difference between the appearance of the male and the female. The female lays eggs at random and these may take up to six months to hatch.

Should be kept in: a large tank with a warm light bulb or (ideally) a locust cage. Newly hatched young may be kept in jars or caterpillar cylinders.
At a temperature of: 70°F (ideal) minimum 50°F.
Food: Bramble.
Notes: Daily spraying with a fine mist spray of water is recommended.

Australian stick insects have a three-stage life cycle. They must have sufficient space in their container to accommodate skin change. Adults may live for between one and two years.

Foreign moths

A wide range of species is available and suppliers will provide information about those which are relatively easy to breed and their native lands. Certainly the exotic silk moths are colourful, spectacular and not difficult.

Should be kept in: insect cylinders, small aquaria or large jars. Adults need plenty of space to accommodate their wing span. Containers should be ventilated.
At a temperature of: a 'normal' room.
Food: This varies depending on the species – check when ordering supplies.
Notes: Moths have a four-stage life cycle (egg, larva, pupa, adult). The larva phase in particular requires a great deal of attention and enthusiasm – large amounts of food will be consumed daily. Adults require almost no maintenance. Anyone considering cultivation of moths is urged to consult books on specific species.
NB Butterflies are well worth attempting but are generally more difficult to breed.

Locusts (from arid areas)

These are large, fascinating insects, relatively easy to keep. Two species are commonly available.

Should be kept in: a specially designed locust cage with light bulb for warmth and sand tubes for egg laying. Other containers/tanks may be adapted.
At a temperature of: 70°F.
Food: Ideally sprouted wheat (growing this is a good project for the classroom). Otherwise, they will eat most green leaves (grass, lettuce, cabbage). Bran is a good optional extra.
Notes: Locusts mate frequently and for prolonged periods. Eggs are laid in sand tubes in cage. These may be incubated and will hatch after 11 days at 30°C. Locusts have a three-stage life cycle. Birth and death rates are high. The adult only lives for about three months. Food must be supplied daily (it will be consumed at a great rate) and cleanliness is important.

Praying mantis (from tropical lands)

A large, spectacular insect, fascinating for many reasons not least among them being its carnivorous habit. It is not easy to rear, but worth the effort of trying.

Should be kept in: large jars or cylinders. Each insect must be housed on its own! Space is essential for skin change. There should be a twig or small branch to act as a 'perch'.

At a temperature of: 60–70°F.

Food: Live insects, e.g. blowflies. Newly hatched nymphs should be fed on small prey, e.g. fruit flies.

Notes: A praying mantis has a three-stage life cycle. For breeding, a large cage is needed, containing leafy branches. The female should be well fed before introducing the male! Mating will occur if the male is placed on the back of the female. They may be left together overnight but should be separated the next morning. When the female produces her fertilised eggs they should be kept in a humid container at a temperature of around 30°C. Nymphs should hatch in three weeks. When in their third instar the young should be separated into individual containers.

African giant land snails

It is essential to ensure that your supplies have been reared in this country (imported snails may carry disease). They are absolutely fascinating creatures. Children will be amazed at their colossal size compared to garden snails.

Should be kept in: a plastic aquarium or similar. Light is not essential so a plastic 'box-like' container with lid is fine. It should, of course, have ventilation. The bottom of the container should have a layer of peat, moss or moist leaves. A broken flower pot (clay) or piece of bark should also be included so that the snails can hide.

At a temperature of: 70°F (will hibernate at lower temperature).

Food: Lettuce, apple slices and other green food. Cuttlefish bone is also essential (for the snails to build their shells).

Notes: Food should be changed regularly and the container should be kept humid by spraying with a fine mist spray. The whole container should be cleaned out every week or so. Two snails (hermaphrodite) are required for breeding so that fertilisation will occur. Eggs are laid in the moist litter which will hatch into young snails. It will take around two years for them to reach full size.

Giant millepedes

As with the African snails, these are well worth keeping as their size and 'wave-like' movement patterns will be sources of fascination and amazement.

Should be kept in: a plastic tank (with lid) or a large bucket. The base should be peat litter and bark should be provided for sheltering beneath.

At a temperature of: 70°F.

Food: Lettuce, slices of apple and other green food. This should be replenished regularly so that it is always fresh.
Notes: Breeding occurs within a special segment, without legs, which contains the reproductive organs. Eggs are laid which hatch into young millepedes. As they grow they shed their skins regularly.

Suppliers of invertebrate and/or housing

(Catalogues available on request)

Blades Biological
Scarletts Oast
Furnace Lane
Edenbridge
Kent TN8 7EG

Entomological Livestock Supplies
Unit 3
Beaver Park
Hayseech Road
Halesowen
West Midlands B63 3PZ

Philip Harris Biological Ltd
Biological Suppliers
Lynn Lane
Shenstone
Lichfield
Staffordshire WS14 0EE

4 ORGANISING GEOGRAPHICAL EDUCATION: A WHOLE-SCHOOL APPROACH

Background

This case study is provided by Newtown Infant School, Stockton, Cleveland, an inner-city school built in 1906 with 264 pupils on the roll plus a 39-place nursery. Staffing is as follows:
Head teacher
Deputy head teacher
Ten class teachers
One head of nursery, one nursery teacher, two NNEB, two and a half auxiliaries.

Geography is co-ordinated by a rate B teacher who has responsibility for history, geography and environmental work throughout the school. It is the purpose of the case study to show how this particular school team has organised its policy and approach to the teaching of early years geographical education. Basically, this is focused on three levels of documentation: a school policy statement, a booklet for guidance on the teaching of geography, and specific plans for topic work throughout the school.

Policy statement: a) for the school booklet, issued to parents, governors, LEA and staff

Geography

Geography is all around us. We hope to make the children aware of this and help them to make sense of the world. Through topics the children learn that there is a relationship between people and places, and that they themselves have an influence on the environment whether it be at a local, national or international level.

The starting point for the children is looking at their local environment, first the home and school, and then beyond that into the immediate locality. From there we aim to help the children acquire an awareness of the world, linking other countries with artefacts so making it as real as possible. Whenever possible learning is through first-hand experience but other media, such as displays, books, films, newspapers, TV programmes, tapes and slides, etc., are used to aid learning and start the enquiry process.

Topics include: food and farming, transport, building, weather and climate, seas and rivers, the home area, people and places, holidays. We aim to increase the children's environmental awareness, looking at environmental issues because today we all have a responsibility which should be recognised.

Environmental issues include: water pollution, air pollution, litter and waste, endangered species, destruction of the rain forest. Because of the growing concern for the environment and nature conservation, we hope to kindle an interest in all age groups in wildlife by creating a nature reserve in the school grounds, giving children a chance to experience nature and wildlife at first hand.

Policy statement: b) for the school staff

Geography: a school policy

Geography incorporates the exploration and understanding of the children's surroundings and the world in which we live.

It is most important to stimulate their enquiring minds, make them aware of our world on a physical and human level, and satisfy their growing need to 'know the reason why'. Whenever possible geography is made real to the children by offering opportunities for direct experience, practical activities and exploration.

Aims and objectives

Children should develop their knowledge and understanding of places in local, regional, national, international and global contexts. They should develop knowledge and understanding of the physical element of geography including weather and climate, water forms, landforms, animal and plant life. Children should also develop their knowledge and understanding of human geography looking at populations, settlements and communications.

Environmental geography also plays a part in their understanding of the world and should include the use and misuse of natural resources, the quality and vulnerability of different environments and the possibilities of protecting and managing environments.

Content

Geographical skills

Enquiry forms an important part of children's work. Consequently, their own interest, experiences and capabilities are taken into account and lead to investigations based on fieldwork and classroom activities.

Places

Pupils develop their awareness of localities in and beyond their own country. Children build on their own experiences from visits but secondary sources are also used such as photographs, objects, stories, video, and accounts by teachers and other adults.

We look at:

1   where the children live;
2   the locality of the school;
3   a locality in the UK which offers a contrast to the school area; and
4   a locality beyond the UK.

Physical geography

Children investigate the natural environment such as soil, water and rocks, and study landscape features. They investigate weather conditions and patterns locally and in different parts of the world.

Human geography

Children investigate the uses made of buildings in the local area and farther afield. People and journeys are looked at as well as adults and their work.

Environmental geography

Children discuss and explain likes and dislikes about their environment and consider ways in which they can improve their own environment.

Environmental geography also includes natural resources and where they come from, compared with manufactured goods.

All these areas of study are covered under the umbrella of topic work in the classroom where geography is integrated into the whole curriculum, e.g. me/my world/houses and buildings/seasons/transport/holidays/water. In addition, geography through story has a large contribution to the input of this curriculum area as well as daily talking and listening sessions in the classroom.

The school provides a variety of resources to help children learn and investigate: TV programmes, cassettes, IT, globes, atlases, maps, charts, plans, floor maps, videos, photographs, postcards, reference books, story books. We also invite visitors into school to speak, e.g. the local policeman, the school nurse, a charity organisation.

Educational visits are made both locally and farther afield in support of topics looked at in the classroom.

Projects which the children are continually involved in include the improvement of their own school grounds, contact with the local community, the Walk for Wildlife and other animal charities in the UK.

Booklet for guidance

A helpful booklet has been put together by the head teacher, the deputy head and the curriculum co-ordinator, entitled *Geography with Infants*.

This is intended to be of general use in the teaching of geography, irrespective of the specific topics being undertaken. It contains suggested activities and guidance for each attainment target, plus lists of relevant computer programs, story books, non-fiction books and teacher resource books. Many of its resource ideas are incorporated in Chapter 7. Some of the suggested activities and examples of children's work relating to the attainment targets of the original geography Order (readily transferable to the geographical content of any topic) are provided below.

Geography with Infants

'Wow'ee, look here's our school and there's
our classroom and there's me inside, looking
at a map with our school on it and . . .'

Introduction

Geography is all around us. We hope to make the children aware of this and help them to make sense of the world. Through topics the children learn that there is a relationship between people and places, and that they themselves have an influence on the environment, whether it be at a local, national or international level.

Above all:

GEOGRAPHY IS FUN!

This booklet offers workable ideas, activities and experiences from the children at Newtown Infant School which have proved fun and valuable.

Whenever possible, learning is through first-hand experience, but other media such as displays, books, films, newspapers, TV programmes, tapes, slides, etc., are used to aid learning and start the enquiry process.

We hope that you will find some useful ideas to help you in the classroom and we are only too glad to share them with you.

AT1   Geographical skills

1 Use of coloured arrows around the school to help children/visitors find their way to the office, head teacher's room, nursery, etc.
2 Use of coloured arrows in the classroom to help children identify various areas, e.g. story corner, writing corner, etc.
3 Set up a travel agency within the classroom.
4 Model farms/zoos, etc. Make workcards/language master cards for the children to use when they play with the animals and buildings. The instructions should use directional words and help the children to construct the model, e.g. put the cow in front of the tree, etc.

5 Children to fill in distance circles showing their own perception of near and far without any teacher intervention!
6 Children to make a plan of their school pet's home.
7 Children to make their own plans of the classroom.
8 Children to draw a bird's eye view of a single object.
9 Children to make models, then draw round them and look at the shape.
10 Children to go on to make plans of the school and the local area. Refer to plans and maps in books and atlases.
11 In talking and listening time talk about where the children have been in the local environment.
12 Children can make a plan of their journey to school.
13 Make a magnetic journey. A child draws a map on card, e.g. the gingerbread boy's journey. Draw and cut out a gingerbread boy and put a paper clip on him. Use a magnet under the map to follow his journey.
14 Co-ordinates can be introduced through story, e.g. a story about pirates would lead the children to draw a map of an island. Put letters across the top (maximum of ten) and numbers down the side. Finding the treasure or shipwreck will help to give an early concept of co-ordinates.
15 A large compass, map and games painted on the playground will not only improve the school environment but can give an early introduction to orienteering. Teachers and/or children can devise different routes to be followed.
16 Use an assortment of commercial/teacher-/child-made weather charts and records.
17 Build up an assortment of photographs and pictures which show geographical features.
18 There should be progression in each year group of how the weather is recorded.
19 Teacher-/child-made weather symbols to be used in all recording.
20 Build up a collection of postcards/photographs of mountains, towns and beaches. Put the appropriate

vocabulary on language master cards and the children can match words to pictures.
21 A set of shoe boxes with labels on saying Towns, Mountains and Beaches could be used to sort the photographs/postcards.

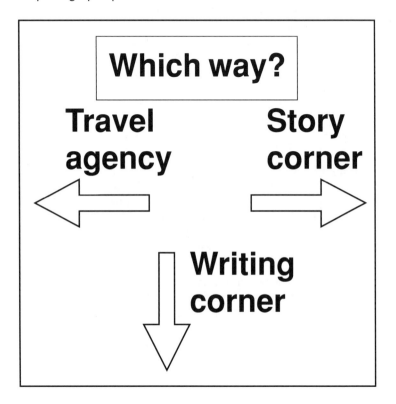

AT2 Knowledge and understanding of places

1 Start within the school with people who help us, e.g. dinner ladies, caretaker, teachers, etc., then work outwards.

**Setting up a 'TRAVEL AGENCY' on a budget!
It's so easy!**

SUGGESTIONS	WHERE FROM?

Travel brochures
        magazines
        leaflets
        tourist guides
        maps
	Travel agencies:
	    Thomas Cook
	    Lunn Poly
	    Callers-Pegasus, etc.
	    Tourist Information Centre

Selection of books	School reference library Local library
Brochures on local excursions	Tourist Information Centre
Guided tours	Art galleries Museums Libraries Free newspapers
Posters	Travel agencies Tourist Information Office
Official passport forms	Post Office
Telephone	Old telephones (British Telecom) (Ask staff/parents)
Yellow Pages Telephone Directory	Old ones from secretary's office or from home
Assortment of stationery	Stock cupboard
Globe, wallcharts	Possibly new stock to order
Postcards	Children/staff send to school
Airline tickets, bus and ferry tickets, luggage labels, ticket wallets and foreign currency	Own/friends'/relatives'/ holidays
Diary – current year and wallplanner	New to order
Booking forms	Devise own format or use back of travel brochures

School crossing patrol
Local policeman
School nurse

Build up resources of pictures, books, jigsaws, etc.

2 Use a book, such as Ahlberg's *Jolly Postman*, as a resource to introduce knowledge of home address.

3 Display of three bears' address in public area in school. Get the children to invent addresses for different animals.

4 Display large school address in the entrance hall for the children to consult.

5 House numbers – make a frieze of the children's front doors, paying special attention to the number.

6 Class letter box for real use – party invitations, etc., posted in envelopes with the children's addresses written on.

7 Make a class or group book of holiday experiences – to encourage children to send postcards to the school when they are on holiday and collect postcards of their visits.

8 Use waxed playmats/wallcharts of the British Isles/world. Jigsaws. Inflatable globes.

9 Set up wildlife park/zoo within the classroom using Playmobil/Lego and models. Inflatable animal globe. Children to bring own soft toys for display. Sorting activities, e.g. Which ones come from this country? Which ones come from abroad? Hot countries/cold countries? Land/water? Can also use the children themselves, given animals' names and playing sorting games in hall.

10 Links through whole-school displays and assemblies, e.g. harvests from other countries, music, food. Displays of artefacts from other countries linking in with topics, e.g. materials and clothing.

11 Encourage the children to enjoy using real phrases and words from other countries daily in the classroom.

12 Build up a collection of children's books from abroad written in foreign languages.

13 Make large class books: 'Our links with Cleveland', 'Our

links with the UK', 'Our links with the world'. Children to include their own written accounts and match with photocopy of National Curriculum maps.

14 Use story books, e.g. *Balloon for Grandad*. Teasel board activities – characters and features.

15 Links with another school in UK and abroad.

AT3 *Physical geography*

1 Geology with infants! Yes, this is possible through topic work such as dinosaurs, mini-beasts, weather/weathering, water, building materials and farming.

2 Build up your own rock collection by getting samples from beaches (must be well cleaned). Young children are fascinated by rocks and this can result in some excellent language work. Always have a magnifying glass available.

3 Make a sediment sorting bottle. This simple device fascinates children and demonstrates the process of deposition, sedimentation and graded bedding found in deep seas, lakes and river flood plains. It can be used to show how sandstones, mudstones, limestones, shales, etc., are formed by particles settling under water. Take a large two-litre plastic lemonade bottle and place approximately half a cupful each of coarse gravel, fine gravel, coarse sand, fine sand, soil and clay into the bottle and fill to the top with tap water. Secure with electrical tape for safety and shake – carefully! Leave to settle for two to three days. Coarse gravel should be at the bottom, then fine gravel, then coarse sand, fine sand, soil particles, and finally clay.

4 Make your own rocks. When children understand how sediment is sorted, samples of the gravel, sand, soil and clay can be made into rocks. You can make rocks using:

Material	Rock type
Coarse sand	Gritstone
Sand	Sandstone
Small pebbles	Conglomerate
Soil/Mud	Shale
White clay	Limestone
Brown clay	Mudstone

Three-quarters fill a yogurt or margarine pot with your rock material. Add two or three teaspoons of Polyfilla and a small amount of water to make a stiff paste. Leave to dry. When dry remove from pot. A sediment profile can be made from the sediment bottle experiment, by placing coarse sediments at the bottom and fine sediments at the top.

5 Make a model volcano by using cardboard, modelling clay or papier mâché. A steep-sided cone works best. In the top of the volcano place a small pot or lid. The lava mixture is made from sodium bicarbonate, vinegar and a few drops of cochineal. When these are mixed together in the top of the cone, the red 'lava' slowly oozes down the sides of the volcano. When the 'lava' dries, drawings can be made of the lava flow patterns. It is very spectacular!

6 Dress a cut-out doll or character in seasonal clothing.

7 Season sequencing. The children draw a picture of the four seasons on separate pieces of paper and put them in order.

8 Take photographs of the same scene outside school in the different seasons.

9 The children draw a seasonal scene. Then draw and cut out figures dressed for spring, summer, autumn and winter. Laminate scenes and figures. Groups of children can then place the figures on the correct season.

10 Make a large frieze showing the water cycle.

AT4 Human geography

1 Make a map of the local shopping area. The children to put photograph in correct position. Zigzag book of shops with an activity showing what produce is bought at each shop. Match photograph of shopkeeper with shop.
2 Build up resources of commercially produced photographs to encourage oral work. Compare buildings and homes in different countries.
3 Make a model in Technology of a car/bus/taxi, etc., and then produce own three-dimensional version of journey, including models of different types of building, e.g. church, house, office block.
Make three-dimensional models/maps of journeys using story books as stimulus, e.g.

   Postman Pat
   Goldilocks and the Three Bears
   The Three Little Pigs
   The Three Billy Goats Gruff
   Town Mouse and Country Mouse
   On the Way Home
   Lily Takes a Walk

4 Make a journey to school survey.
5 Make a holiday survey. Holiday journeys – display of postcards and how travelled.
6 Go on outdoor walks and journeys looking at buildings to compare and contrast.
7 Talk about famous journeys that people have made and why.
8 People who help us – jigsaws.
Role play area – hospital ward, estate agent's, shop.
9 Children make and colour large floor map of local area and site nearest hospital. Make DT models of ambulances and use to find addresses and return journeys to hospital on map.

10 Visits and talks by local people, and people involved with school. Adopt a shop.

AT5 *Environmental geography*

1 Form a friendship with a school in a different setting to yours and exchange visits.
2 Take children on outings/visits to different environments.
3 Group and class discussions about likes and dislikes of local area. Children could fill in an individual tick list on a scale of one to ten. Children could make a town guide.
4 Make use of any areas within the school grounds (no matter how small) to promote conservation and wildlife – sense garden, herb garden, bog garden, pond, wild flower garden, log pile, etc.
5 Sensory trails, sensory walks, find and feel.
6 Displays of natural resources, e.g. wood, stone, cotton, wool, to touch and discuss.
7 Make a clothes shop – label goods and materials.
8 Food from different places. Matching foods and produce with materials of origin.
9 Mobiles and sorting activities: things from under the ground; things from the sea; things from trees; things from farms.
10 Collection of pictures of natural environments and man-made environments. Talking points. Sorting activities.
11 Environmental issues: conservation and endangered species; pollution – pollution walk identifying different kinds of pollution; waste; recycling – locate bottle banks, save-a-can scheme, paperchase; noise – survey with scale, recordings; litter – weekly womble scheme around school.

Topic work

Beyond the levels of whole-school policy and guidance in the form of suggested activities and resources, teaching teams engage in the planning of general topics which include discernible elements of geographical education. It is intended that the booklet for guidance is used alongside these topics. The school staff have made the collective decision that the topic-work approach is the appropriate method of including the foundation subjects in the curriculum. Topics change each term for most classes – or every half-term in the case of Reception children. Overall planning for topics takes place at school level. The staff come together and decide on a year plan of themes as shown in Figure 4.8. An extended version of this is then produced, linking themes with the main attainment targets to be covered. The school's three staff teams, i.e. Nursery/Reception, year 1 and year 2 teaching teams then meet to brainstorm and plan topic webs based on the specific topic that they will be teaching for the term. Figure 4.9 shows the topic web for the theme 'Inside Outside' planned by the year 2 team. The next stage of planning involves consultation with the geography co-ordinator, who provides input by suggesting ideas for incorporating worthwhile geography into the topic. She also helps with the provision of resources. Completed plans (linked to attainment targets) and specific requests for additional resources go back to the head teacher for comment, and are circulated to the whole staff. From time to time, staff meetings are held to monitor and review the progress of all topics, and the geography co-ordinator maintains an overview of the implementation of National Curriculum geography in practice.

Assessment

The staff at Newtown Infant School place great emphasis on the importance of oral assessment in geography rather than merely focusing on testing the acquisition of skills. Thus they pay much attention to listening, observing and questioning, in line with the emphasis given in Chapter 5. Such oral assessment begins at the earliest stage, i.e. in the Reception class. Pupil records in geography have traditionally been maintained on individual sheets which specify the topics which a child has covered. Formal record-keeping charts are currently being updated to take account of specific National Curriculum attainment targets. Individual child profiles are also maintained. Samples of work are kept which contribute to an overall folio of achievement in geography. Three examples of such work are given below. These are representative of work completed by year 2 children in their studies of a locality beyond the UK (see Figures 4.10, 4.11 and 4.12).

	Autumn		Spring		Summer	
Reception	Colour		Water	Changes (including growth, animal homes)	Patterns (including shadow and reflection)	Journeys (including energy)
Year 1	Circles and spheres (including Earth and space)	Food and celebrations (including electricity and light)	Textiles — Pattern (including insulation)	Colour (including sight and touch)	Opposites (including transport)	Toys (including forces and air)
Year 2	Inside and outside (including electricity and magnetism)	(including fabrics and structures)	Use and misuse of the environment (including good health)	(including hearing, smell, taste)	On the move (including floating and sinking)	(including sound and music)

Figure 4.8 Newtown Infant School – themes

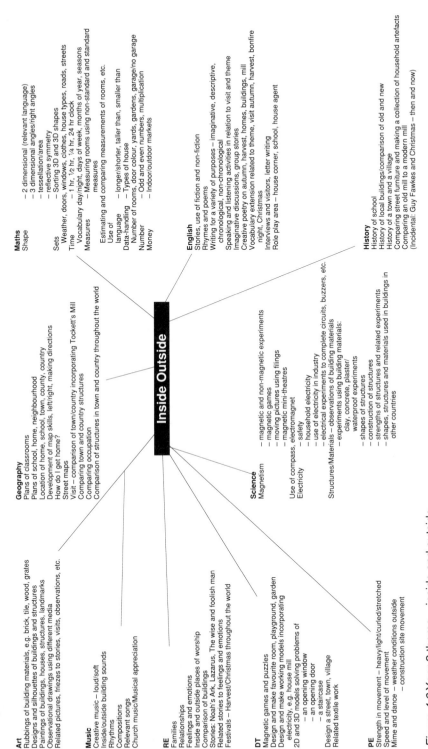

Art
Rubbings of building materials, e.g. brick, tile, wood, grates
Designs and silhouettes of buildings and structures
Paintings of buildings, houses, structures, landmarks
Observational drawings using different media
Related pictures, friezes to stories, visits, observations, etc.

Music
Creative music – loud/soft
Inside/outside building sounds
Rhythms
Compositions
Relevant songs
Church music/Musical appreciation

RE
Families
Relationships
Feelings and emotions
Inside and outside places of worship
Comparison of buildings
Stories: Noah's Ark, Lazarus, The wise and foolish man
Related stories to feelings and emotions
Festivals – Harvest/Christmas throughout the world

DT
Magnetic games and puzzles
Design and make favourite room, playground, garden
Design and make working models incorporating
  electricity, e.g. house mill
2D and 3D models solving problems of
  – an opening window
  – an opening door
  – a staircase
Design a street, town, village
Related textile work

PE
Strength in movement – heavy/light/curled/stretched
Speed and level of movement
Mime and dance – weather conditions outside
  – construction site movement

Geography
Plans of classrooms
Plans of school, home, neighbourhood
Location of home, school, town, county, country
Development of map skills, left/right, making directions
How do I get home?
Street maps
Visit – comparison of town/country incorporating Tockett's Mill
Comparing town and country structures
Comparing occupation
Comparison of structures in town and country throughout the world

Science
Magnetism   – magnetic and non-magnetic experiments
             – magnetic games
             – moving pictures using filings
             – magnetic mini-theatres
Use of compass, electromagnet
Electricity – safety
             – household electricity
             – use of electricity in industry
             – electrical experiments to complete circuits, buzzers, etc.
Structures/Materials – observations of building materials
             – experiments using building materials:
               clay, concrete, plaster/
               waterproof experiments
             – shapes of structures
             – construction of structures
             – strengths of structures and related experiments
             – shapes, structures and materials used in buildings in
               other countries

Inside Outside

Maths
Shape   – 2 dimensional (relevant language)
             – 3 dimensional angles/right angles
             – tessellation/area
             – reflective symmetry
Sets   – Sorting 3D and 3D shapes
Weather, doors, windows, clothes, house types, roads, streets
Time   – 1 hr, ½ hr, ¼ hr, 24 hr clock
Vocabulary day/night, days of week, months of year, seasons
Measures   – Measuring rooms using non-standard and standard
               measures
Estimating and comparing measurements of rooms, etc.
Use of
language   – longer/shorter, taller than, smaller than
Data-handling – Types of house
Number of rooms, door colour, yards, gardens, garage/no garage
Number   – Odd and even numbers, multiplication
Money   – Indoor/outdoor markets

English
Stories, use of fiction and non-fiction
Rhymes and poems
Writing for a variety of purposes – imaginative, descriptive,
  chronological, non-chronological
Speaking and listening activities in relation to visit and theme
Imaginative discussions, group stories
Creative poetry on autumn, harvest, homes, buildings, mill
Vocabulary extension related to theme, visit autumn, harvest, bonfire
  night, Christmas
Interviews and visitors, letter writing
Role play area – house corner, school, house agent

History
History of school
History of local buildings/comparison of old and new
History of a town and a village
Comparing street furniture and making a collection of household artefacts
Comparing an old mill to a modern mill
(Incidental: Guy Fawkes and Christmas – then and now)

Figure 4.9 Year 2 theme – inside and outside

3

Wednesday II th November 1992

Japan   is far-away   more
   than   stockton   and   china
      The   sea   is   all   round   it
   In , Japan   they   eat   with
      chopsticks   and   they
      bow They   go   to   school
         and   take   a   packed
         lunch I   do   as   well.

Michelle

Figure 4.10   Work sample (a) contributing to geographical portfolio

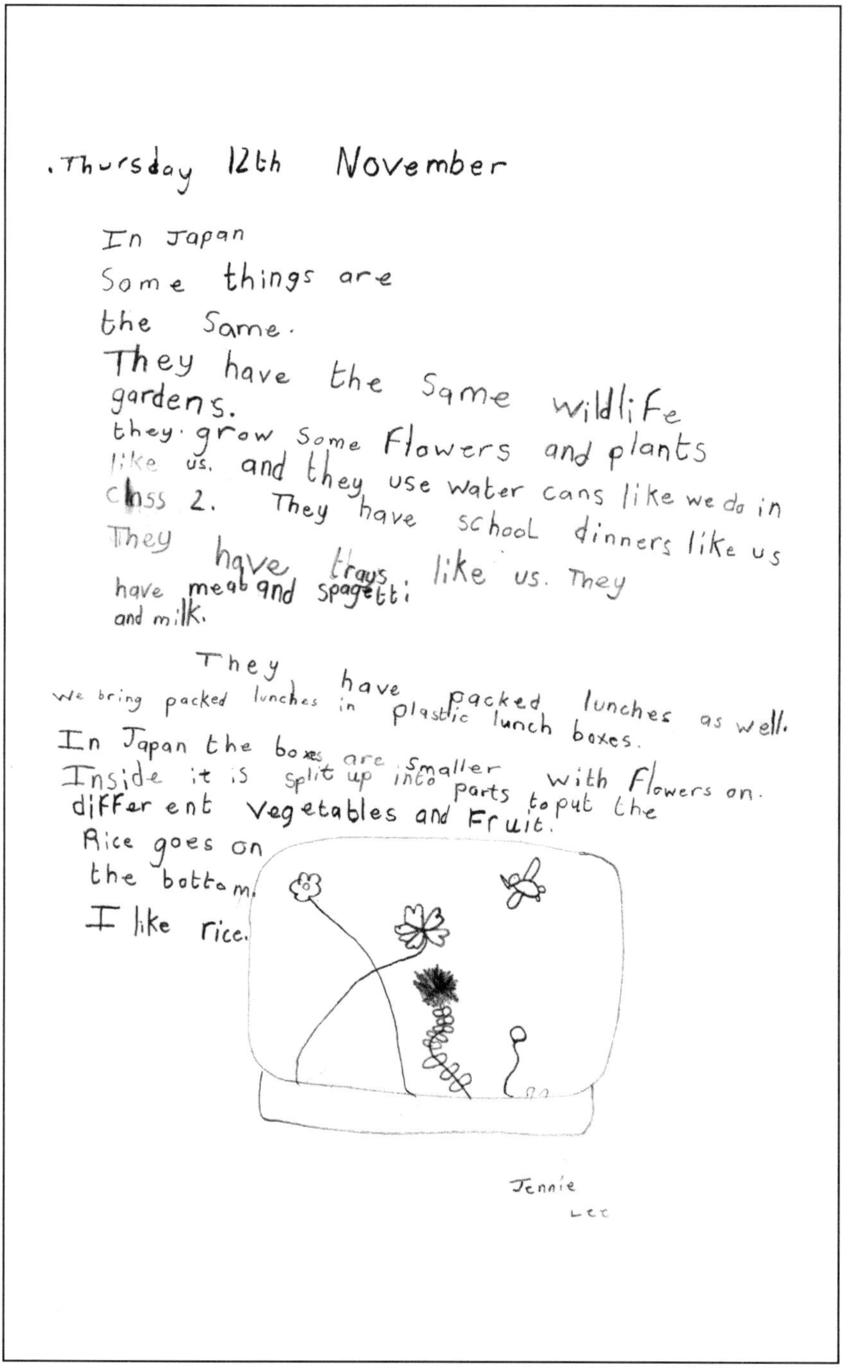

.Thursday 12th November

In Japan
Some things are
the Same.
They have the Same wildlife
gardens.
they grow Some Flowers and plants
like us. and they use water cans like we do in
class 2.   They have school dinners like us
They have trays, like us. They
have meat and spagetti
and milk.

They have packed lunches
We bring packed lunches in plastic lunch boxes as well.
In Japan the boxes are smaller
Inside it is split up into different parts with flowers on.
different Vegetables and Fruit to put the
Rice goes on
the bottom.
I like rice.

Jennie
Lee

Figure 4.11   Work sample (b) contributing to geographical portfolio

Thursday 12th November

In Japan

Same things are

the Same.
they have the Same P.E.

they av the Same dinner time The girls give
aut the diners but we have nannies.
they do pictures
and they eat with chopsticks
they eat a lot of rice
and they have raw eggs I wil not Like raw eggs.

Zoé M<Lennell

A house in Japan

Figure 4.12   Work sample (c) contributing to geographical portfolio

5 THE USE OF STORY

This study shows how a single story, commonly found in early years classrooms, can form the basis for exciting and worthwhile geographical education. The teacher in question took as a starting point the story entitled *Red Fox* by H. Giffard (Frances Lincoln, ISBN 0–7112–0747–X). Preparation involved an analysis of the story in terms of its potential for geographical work, identified page by page throughout the book, and recorded as a list of geographical language that could be developed, links with attainment targets and levels of attainment, and the potential of illustrations. This analysis is summarised below (linking with attainment targets of the original Order).

The story was then read to the children and the geographical potential as outlined was developed through discussion of text and illustrations, and related tasks. One key task, for example, involved the children in drawing their own spontaneous maps of the journey of the fox.

Analysis of story: its potential for geographical education

Red Fox

Briefly, this story describes the journey of a fox setting off in search of his food. The story is initially set in the countryside, starting at the fox's den in woodlands; however, as the fox searches further afield for his food he ends up in a town. In the story, therefore, children are introduced to the contrast between rural and urban areas. Furthermore, the fox's journey passes a variety of different places, and is a good starting point for developing children's mapping skills, encouraging children to remember all the different places that the fox has passed.

Let us now turn to an analysis of the book's geographical content in terms of its language and pictures, and then see how the geography attainment targets are addressed. The analysis has been carried out page by page, in the following manner:

Page 1
1 *Language*
   'over the faraway hills' = direction/distance vocabulary.
   'hills' = geographical features.
   'den'

Page 2
1 *Language*
   'stay here' = locational language.
   'I'll find something to eat' = setting the scene for the journey.

2   *Picture* – countryside scene
  woods
  hills – reinforcing the children's understanding of these.
  den = geographical feature.

Page 3
1   *Language*
  'headed for' = directional language.
  'farm' = geographical feature – recognising that different buildings have different purposes.
  'farmer' = indicating that adults do different kinds of work.
2   *Picture*
  woodland/hills/yard/buildings for different purposes – reinforcing understanding and geographical features.

Page 5 – 'red fox ran off towards the pond . . .'
1   *Language*
  'off towards' = directional language.
  'pond' = geographical feature – recognising the different ways in which water occurs in the environment.
2   *Picture*
  see the farm buildings near to the pond.

Page 7 – 'He heard a faint rustling in the corn field nearby.'
1   *Language*
  'corn field' = geographical feature.
  'nearby' = locational language.
2   *Picture*
  wheat field with a woodland in the background, therefore helps to reinforce children's understanding of different land uses.

Page 10
1   *Language*
  'behind the glowing moon' = locational language.
  'Then he heard a scuffling at the edge of the wood'
  'edge' = locational language.
  'wood' = geographical feature.
  '. . . he sprang towards the noise . . .' = directional language.
  'across' = directional language.
  'field' = geographical feature.
  'Red fox chased him down to the railway line'
  'down to' = directional language.
  'the railway line' = geographical feature – illustrating different modes of transport.

2 *Picture*
   woods/hill field = reinforcing the geographical features introduced in the text.

Page 11

1 *Language*
   'a fast train came round the bend'
   'round the bend' – directional language.

2 *Picture*
   fields with cows grazing = illustrating another land use in the country-side.

Page 12

1 *Language*
   'up the bank' = directional language.
   'bank' = geographical feature.

2 *Picture*
   railway track and train.
   steep bank with sheep grazing.
   woods – recognising different relief in land.

Page 13

1 *Language*
   'Red fox went to the river'
   'went to' = directional language.
   'the river' = geographical feature – illustrating another term in which water occurs in the environment.
   '. . . reflections from a nearby town'
   'nearby' = locational language.
   'town' = geographical feature.

2 *Picture*
   hill, river, town at edge of picture, thus indicating its 'nearby' position.

Page 15

1 *Language*
   'The huge buildings' = reinforcing the idea that different buildings have different purposes.
   'the streets' = geographical feature.

2 *Picture* showing a typical town scene, therefore is quite a contrast to the earlier scene of the countryside.

Page 17

1 *Language*
   'turned a corner' = directional language.

'narrow street' = geographical feature.

'across a yard' = directional language.

2 *Picture*

Urban setting outside a home, again showing a contrast with the fox's home at the beginning of the story.

Page 19

1 *Language*

'home' = geographical feature.

'across' = directional language.

'the fields' = geographical feature.

2 *Picture*

Fox leaving the town and re-entering the countryside, therefore a direct contrast between the two places is seen.

It is evident that this story book introduces many geographical features, reinforced in the pictures, which should enable the children to understand the geographical terms more fully and, perhaps more important, it provides a more meaningful content. After the geographical content had been analysed in terms of both the language and pictures, the teacher looked to see how the geographical content addressed the geography attainment targets. This information has been summarised as follows.

Teacher's evaluation

The work carried out with this book involved year 1 children. I felt that the children enjoyed the story as they were enthusiastic when discussing it. Similarly, I felt that they enjoyed focusing on the illustrations as they picked out the geographical features they had heard about in the text and pointed them out. This showed that the children had a good understanding of these terms, e.g. wood, field, pond, river and farm. Indeed, children seem to gain a much better understanding of things when they see them in pictures; undoubtedly, it helps them to put things into more meaningful contexts. Thus, these children demonstrated that they could use geographical vocabulary to talk about places – AT1 level 2a – and furthermore were able to identify these features in the pictures.

The book was especially helpful in stimulating discussion about the countryside. The children contrasted the countryside and the town. One child, for example, described the countryside as 'green and quiet', whereas she said the town was 'grey and smoky and busy'. It was interesting to hear what the children thought about these two contrasting places. As all the children lived in a town, they found it easy to describe towns through their own personal experiences. However, they all seemed to have a good understanding of the countryside, especially since quite a few of them had never had any direct experience. It seemed that they had picked up most

AT1: GEOGRAPHICAL SKILLS

Level 2a: use geographical vocabulary to talk about places – encourage the children to use the geographical features in the text – hills, den, fields, woods, pond, bank, river, town, street, farm.

Level 2b: make a representation of an imaginary place – the children can be encouraged to plot Red Fox's journey.

Level 2c: identify familiar features in pictures – the geographical features named above can be pointed out in the pictures.

AT5: ENVIRONMENTAL GEOGRAPHY

Level 1b: express personal likes and dislikes about features of the local area – the children could be encouraged to contrast town and country areas, perhaps indicating a preference.

RED FOX
By Hannah Giffard

AT4: HUMAN GEOGRAPHY

Level 1a: recognise buildings are used for different purposes. Farm buildings, plus the 'tall buildings' in the town.

Level 1b: describe ways in which people make journeys in the story; see tains and cars.

Level 1c: recognise that adults do different kinds of work, e.g. the 'farmer', p.3.

AT3: PHYSICAL GEOGRAPHY

Level 2b: identify terms in which water occurs in the environment in the text; water is seen to occur in ponds and rivers.

Figure 4.13   Geographical content of *Red Fox*: diagrammatic summary

of their ideas from what they had seen or heard from a variety of sources, and this demonstrates how important and influential these indirect experiences of the world are for children, enabling them to develop and widen their understanding of the world generally.

When we talked about the places that the fox visited, the children seemed to remember nearly all the places that he had passed and, more important, they were able to sequence them. In our discussions, it was evident that the children had picked up the locational language introduced in the story. For example, when they were sequencing the fox's journey, one boy, Duane,

Figure 4.14 Children's mapwork from *Red Fox*: (a) Atif

Figure 4.15 Children's mapwork from *Red Fox*: (b) Louis

Figure 4.16 Children's mapwork from *Red Fox*: (c) Chloe

picked up on the term 'nearby' and said confidently that he could remember that 'the pond was nearby the farm'.

This demonstrated that he had a good understanding of this term. Indeed, I was surprised by just how much detail the children remembered about Red Fox's journey. This was the first book where I had gathered the children's response, and I had previously anticipated that I would have to help the children more. However, when asked which places he had passed, together they covered every feature, showing that they had taken in all these places when they listened to it for the first time.

Having established that the children had a good understanding of all the places visited, I introduced the idea of making a representation of Red Fox's journey. However, before I did this, I had to ensure that the children had a good understanding of the term map. I was surprised to find that the children were all quite familiar with this, and furthermore they described a map as 'something which shows you where things are'. On further questioning, it seemed that they had come across maps in everyday life; for example, they had seen them in towns and in some shops.

Before they started to make their own representations, we briefly discussed what sort of things should be included on the maps. The children realised that they needed to include all the places that the fox had passed. I was also pleased to find that they wanted to distinguish between the countryside and the town.

The maps produced were extremely pleasing (see Figures 4.14, 4.15 and 4.16). It is interesting to note that the maps show all the features in the correct sequence, and that the children have shown these in more symbolic form. It has been suggested by Mills (1986) that young children's maps are likely to be pictorial and that houses are likely to be drawn as 'stereotyped houses'. In these maps, however, the children have moved on from pictorial representation. Additionally, the children have also used colour effectively, green to denote country areas and black for the town areas. This further illustrates that the children distinguish between the two contrasting areas.

I was pleased with the way that the book stimulated the map work, and I felt that these children demonstrated that they had attained AT1 level 2b, making a representation of a real or an imaginary place. This book helped to foster a greater understanding of the countryside as well as promote other geographical knowledge.

General comments on the use of children's literature in geographical work in the early years

These comments are based on trialling and evaluating three story books: *Red Fox*, as discussed above, by H. Giffard (Frances Lincoln, 1991); *The World That Jack Built* by R. Brown (Red Fox Edition, 1991); and *Katie Morag Delivers the Mail* by M. Hedderick (The Bodley Head Ltd, 1985).

Having considered the children's responses to these books, it is appropriate to evaluate the overall findings, in order to assess the effectiveness of children's literature for developing geographical work.

From the responses, it seems that the books generated some valuable discussions with strong geographical elements. The children enjoyed them, and liked sharing their own ideas and experiences, which is something that should be encouraged. If teachers are to use story books as a stimulus for geographical work, it is important that children are given time to discuss the places mentioned. Such discussions are vital if teachers are to get the most out of story books. If questions do not arise naturally, they can be asked about the places and features introduced. In order to make such discussions valuable, it is important to know in advance which things to focus children's attention on. However, from my own experiences, I found that children are generally eager to discuss the places which they have seen and heard about, and this is of great value in using story books.

Furthermore, in the discussions the children demonstrated their understanding of the geographical features introduced. They liked pointing to certain features in the pictures. This made me think that story books could sometimes be used as an informal means of assessing children's geographical understanding. Children could, for example, identify certain geographical features shown in the pictures, and consequently their attainment of AT1 level 2e could be informally assessed.

The stories also encouraged the children to use locational language when discussing the places and features, which showed an understanding of these terms. Locational language is a fundamental part of geography, and it is important that children can describe the location of places and features in relation to other things. Children's understanding of such language came through the discussions, which again highlights their value. The stories appeared to be both a means of developing the children's vocabulary, and an informal means of assessing their understanding.

Additionally, it is evident that certain geography attainment targets can be addressed in some detail. It seems that the books had strong elements of certain attainment targets. For example, *The World That Jack Built* addressed AT5: Environmental Geography in some depth, while *Katie Morag Delivers the Mail* covered more of AT4: Human Geography, as the children saw adults carrying out different occupations. This suggests that it is possible to develop different areas of the geography curriculum through children's literature in some depth. Additionally, children experience 'geographical ideas' in more meaningful contexts.

One attainment target which it is difficult to address directly through children's literature is AT2: Knowledge and Understanding of Places, as this may have an emphasis on the local area in the early years. Yet stories can help in this area too, as a way of introducing ideas about distant lands and foreign cultures. Any experiences which children gain of studying places indirectly will be valuable later on. It is important that children learn to imagine what places are like through such second-hand experiences, and that they learn to use their imaginations in geographical work, as most of the places that they will learn about in their studies will be through indirect experiences. Children's literature is helpful in developing children's ability to create mental images of distant places.

My findings suggest that stories can provide a good stimulus for map-work, as the children are able to represent the places introduced in the story line. This is an especially valuable contribution to learning for, as previously discussed, mapping skills may be introduced and developed from the time when children arrive in school. It is important that children are encouraged to make representations from an early age. By being encouraged to make representations of places, children employ certain map skills, i.e. scaling the places and features down, and deciding how best to represent them. Children will enjoy constructing spontaneous maps – and the story books certainly encouraged this. Also, the children were able to work more with a context than they would normally do if they had just been asked to draw an imaginary map. Similarly, drawing maps from stories enabled them to be more imaginative. The maps drawn from *Katie Morag Delivers the Mail* illustrate this point, as all the children incorporated the same geographical features, but from different perspectives. This sort of flexibility is advantageous as it allows children to develop their mapping skills, without being too constrained by the notion of a 'correct' representation. On the whole, the maps drawn tended to be pictorial; nevertheless, they showed that the children were able to represent the geographical features effectively. Thus the stories provided the children with a good opportunity to develop mapping skills, which is extremely valuable since they should be assessed on this ability at Key Stage 1.

The books also encouraged the children to sequence the geographical features in the discussions, and when they made their representations. This is an important idea in geography as sequencing applies to many geographical processes. It therefore seems desirable that children have the opportunity to develop this idea from an early age.

These general findings suggest that children's literature is an effective way of introducing young children to geographical skills, concepts and vocabulary, and, what is more, is an enjoyable way. The stories seemed to make geographical ideas more accessible, and helped them to develop their map skills and locational awareness – both major elements in the National Curriculum.

6 THINKING ABOUT HOMES

Background

'Homes' is one of the most frequently studied topics in early years class-rooms. The subject is an excellent focus for cross-curricular interpretation, and lends itself splendidly to the coverage of geographical attainment targets. This particular case study describes some activities appropriate for interpretation of this theme with year 1 or year 2 children, which success-fully allow for coverage of ideas relating to the locality and more distant environments, and which cover a range of geographical content. Unlike many topics on the theme, this particular example of good practice places emphasis on thinking and reflection – hence the title 'Thinking about Homes'. Thus the children are actively involved in thinking and making judgements about a range of homes, including their own. Because of this reflective focus, learning links naturally with elements of environmental education. It has to do with thinking about the quality of environments, as well as scientific and geographical accuracy.

Activities

Encourage reflection on the basic idea that all living things, including animal, plant and human life, need a home. Ask the children to sit quietly and close their eyes. Guide them to some imaginary scenes of homes. The following scenarios will be useful, although one would presumably focus on only one at a time:

A

> You are a flower . . . you have beautiful red petals facing the sunshine. Your leaves are bright green and you have a stem reaching down into the ground. The soil is your home . . . your roots hold you firmly in place. You do not move from your home . . . you have everything that you need there. Think about what it feels like to be a flower . . . how does the ground around you feel? . . . Are there other plants living nearby? Do animals and insects come to visit you? How do you get your water and food?

After this scenario has been read while the children are quiet and have their eyes closed, ask them to talk about their reflections – each could describe their flowery neighbours, imaginary visitors, and what it may feel like to derive water and food from the soil.

B

Imagine you are a worm. Try to think what it feels like to be a worm . . . you are slippery and slimy and wriggle your way across the ground and through the soil. You like your home to be dark and damp. You like to wriggle your way to the top (surface) of the soil when it has been raining . . . You do not have arms and legs . . . you do not have fur and feathers . . .

Think about what you might like to eat . . . leaves have fallen on to your home from the trees. . . . Do you like your home? . . . Who do you share it with? Do you have enemies who share your home?

This scenario can obviously be adapted to a wide range of animals and bird life. Follow up the quiet reflective period with time for discussion on what it may feel like to be a worm, or whatever, in a home which is totally different from ours, yet which provides all life's basic needs – food, shelter, etc. There is clearly tremendous scope for elaboration of this concept into discussion about what a range of life needs are expected from a home.

C

Now imagine that you are going into your own home. . . . You have just got home from school. . . . Imagine your front door . . . and you are now going inside . . . think about what you can see as you go through the door. . . . What does it feel like to be home?

Now imagine that you are hungry in your home. . . . Would you go and find some food?. . . Would you ask someone for some food?. . . What might you have? . . .

Now imagine that you are thirsty . . . think about where you find a drink. . . .

Now think about where you go to sleep in your home . . . think of your bed . . . imagine you are climbing into it. . . . What does your bed feel like? What can you see in the room you sleep in? What do you like best about your home? Would you change anything if you could?

This scenario should lead to a great deal of discussion in which the children are helped to realise that they depend very much on their homes for food, warmth, comfort and shelter. (Note that this activity should be treated with sensitivity if there are children in the class from unhappy or problematic homes.)

Having considered a number of scenarios about homes of different kinds, discuss similarities and differences that occur in plant, animal and human homes. Emphasise the fact that every living thing needs food, water, shelter and space in its home. Everything needs one. This could well lead to the production of a wall display, showing homes of different kinds (animal, plant, human) and in different places – both near and distant. To assist this, make a collection of pictures of homes in different places, and discuss their similarities and differences. Suggest that the children draw pictures of where they live to display alongside your 'homes with a difference'. Ask them to show things that they need to live in their drawings. Key questions to discuss as the display is being prepared and assembled include the following:

- Why do people need homes?
- What do homes provide for us?
- Why do animals need homes?
- What do homes provide for animals?
- Why do plants need homes?
- What do homes provide for plants?
- What do homes protect us from?
- Why do people's homes often look different in other lands?
- What makes a 'good' home (for animals, plants, people)?

Extension ideas

Clearly there is tremendous scope for elaboration of these basic ideas into a whole range of geographical and scientific studies. Many will be obvious. The following suggestions provide a useful extension to the 'thinking about homes' basic concept:

- Habitat surveys (trees, woodlands, ponds, hedgerows, walls, etc.).
- Study of your neighbourhood – setting homes in the general context of living in a community. Perhaps this could focus on 'living places' (homes), 'working places', 'playing places' and 'special places'.
- Dwellings – focus on living places of humans in the locality and further afield, considering building materials, size, layout and function. This provides clear links into studies of distant lands. After suitable research and stories, perhaps children can talk or write about a day in the life of a child from another culture, describing how this person lives in his or her home. Focus on range and size of dwellings in our world, as well as differences in building materials, layout and function. Consider, for example, the simple tepee, consisting of skins, poles, pegs, door flap and smoke flap; also the mansion home of some children of Western cultures, complete with as many bathrooms as bedrooms, swimming pool and games room. Ask the children which they would prefer to live in and why; consider whether size is always an advantage. Do they think that a complex home is always better than a simple one?
- Space to live – suggest to the children that every living thing needs a certain amount of space in order to live. Ask them what it would feel like if two classes had to share their classroom; if another ten people moved

into their house. This extension will help children to begin to appreciate a number of important concepts; for example, that a habitat can only sustain a certain number of living things; that overcrowding leads to a decrease in the quality of a human environment; and that increase in the human population leads to problems in our world. This activity could lead to discussion about (and action on) organising your classroom so that space is used in the best possible way for all its occupants, and about the children's 'personal' space which they have in their own homes. Take a walk into the neighbourhood. Ask the children to look out for examples of how families use their space. Do they have gardens? If so, how do they use them? Do they have fences? If so, why? What can we find out about people by looking at their homes and how their space is used? Last, but not least, consider the space of the school environment. Can the children think of ways of improving the use of school space? (For example, plant flowers in dull areas of the grounds; provide more litter bins to keep open spaces clean.) This extension helps to encourage a focus on values and quality of 'home' space – both personal and communal.

Chapter 5

School policy, assessment and record-keeping

SCHOOL POLICY

If geographical work is to be implemented successfully, a 'whole-school' approach is essential. This approach requires the head teacher and staff to engage in consultation which results in the articulation of a set of principles, goals and practical statements which provide overall direction for teaching and learning of the subject. In the first instance, a decision must be made as to whether geography and environmental education are to have separate or linked policy documents. This is a matter for individual schools to decide: perhaps ideally a pair of linked documents is most helpful; that is, a policy for geography, a policy for environmental education and a statement giving practical guidance on the overlap between the two, in terms of content, organisation and resources. Whatever approach to document production is used, the following structure and suggested content should be helpful.

A whole-school policy will have four key components, as shown in Figure 5.1. During whole staff consultation meetings, it will be necessary to decide who will assume responsibility for decision-making. This is inevitably linked to the second policy component concerned with leadership. Someone – maybe the head teacher or agreed curriculum co-ordinator for geography – must assume responsibility for making decisions based on full staff discussion, and for translating these into plans for action. Presumably this leader will accept the task of overseeing the production and implementation of policy documentation and the management of resources, including human resources in the school. Once such leadership and management decisions have been made, attention can focus on the curriculum and the environment of the school itself as a major resource for teaching and learning.

A publication of this kind cannot possibly prescribe the content of an individual school's policy document. Every school is unique in its organisation, needs and resources. It is, however, possible to suggest guidelines on issues which should be the subject of staff discussion and 'flesh out' the

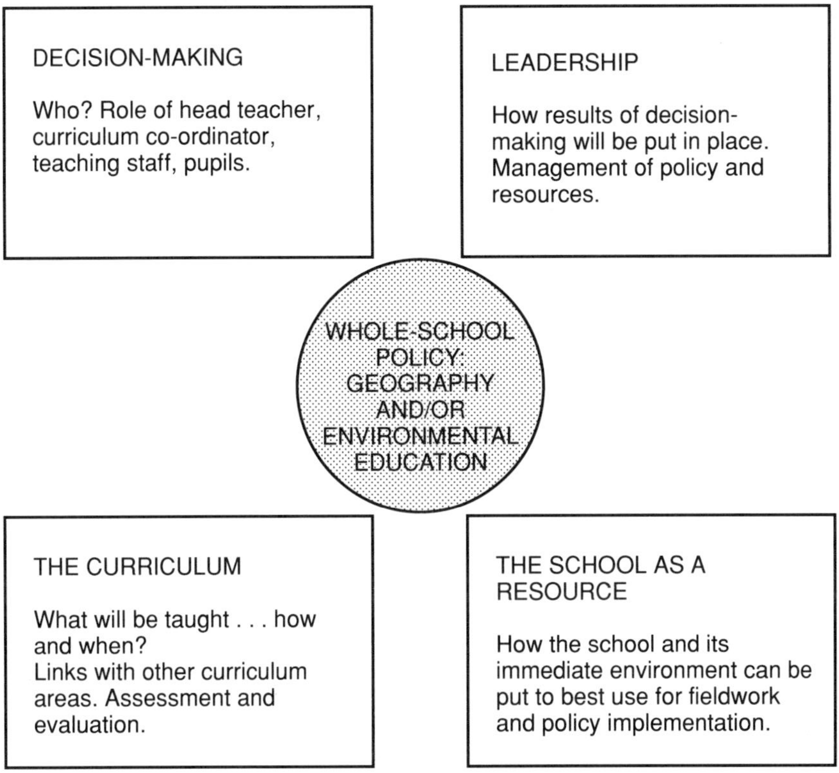

DECISION-MAKING Who? Role of head teacher, curriculum co-ordinator, teaching staff, pupils.	**LEADERSHIP** How results of decision-making will be put in place. Management of policy and resources.
THE CURRICULUM What will be taught . . . how and when? Links with other curriculum areas. Assessment and evaluation.	**THE SCHOOL AS A RESOURCE** How the school and its immediate environment can be put to best use for fieldwork and policy implementation.

WHOLE-SCHOOL POLICY: GEOGRAPHY AND/OR ENVIRONMENTAL EDUCATION

Figure 5.1   Components of a school policy: geography/environmental education

four components indicated in Figure 5.1. The following issues should be addressed:

- What is our school doing already in the areas of geography and environmental education?
- Who is taking the lead in these areas of the curriculum?
- What should we do next?
- How are geography and environmental education set in the context of the curriculum as a whole?
- What is our common school viewpoint that will give consistent approaches to the implementation and organisation of geographical and environmental learning experiences?
- How will time be organised and prioritised?
- How do we achieve a balance between flexibility and the necessary timetable restrictions?

- Do we have adequate facilities for acquisition, storage and distribution of resources?
- How do we ensure curriculum continuity and progression in children's learning in geography?
- How will pupils be grouped and staff deployed for teaching and learning?
- What forms will assessment and record-keeping take?
- How shall we monitor and evaluate geography and environmental education policy in practice?

A formal document deriving from discussion on each of these areas may be subdivided into sections, reflecting the four components of the whole-school approach. As much or as little as the school and staff require may be included under the following headings, conditioned by national legislation and, of course, the existing curriculum statements for the school.

- Decision-making;
- Management and implementation of policy;
- Aims;
- Objectives;
- Methods and timing;
- Content (knowledge, understanding, skills, concepts, attitudes);
- Resources and organisation of resources;
- Assessment, record-keeping and evaluation;
- The school itself as a stimulus for geographical work;
- Other matters (e.g. links with the community, fieldwork, policy for school grounds development and maintenance).

POLICY INTO PRACTICE

Again, a checklist of elaboration on the stages in the implementation of policy may be helpful. Six key stages are essential in the first instance:

1 Organising leadership and communication.
2 Scrutinising the existing programme.
3 Producing a checklist of requirements.
4 Clarifying content and objectives.
5 Providing a rationale for teaching and learning methods.
6 Establishing mechanisms for evaluation, review and development.

A little more will be said about each of these.

Organising leadership and communication

At an appropriate staff meeting, the head teacher will no doubt initiate discussion on leadership for policy implementation. If a curriculum leader for geography and environmental work is already in place (and initiated policy), so far so good. If not, this person must be identified. The implementation phase may well involve the establishment of a working group of staff (especially in larger schools where early years co-ordinators will liaise with colleagues who teach older pupils) who represent different subject areas. This group may also accept responsibility for working and communicating with other interested parties, including parents, the community and the school's governing body. As so much work in geographical and environmental education will require learning outside the classroom, such liaison is essential.

Scrutinising the existing programme

Work already being done in the school will no doubt form the basis for development. Questions to consider are:

1 What schemes, topics, programmes already contribute to geographical and environmental work?
2 Is the answer to the above question comprehensive? What about extra-curricular activities? What about the hidden curriculum? What messages, both formal and informal, do the pupils receive about quality of the school environment and the need to take care of it?
3 What are the existing views of staff, parents, governors, about the place of geography and environmental education in the curriculum?
4 What links already exist between geographical, environmental work and other curriculum areas?
5 Can we identify areas where overlap of content occurs or repetition?
6 What enthusiasm, expertise, experience and resources already exist in the school for teaching geography and environmental education?
7 What enthusiasm, expertise and experience in these areas can be identified among parents and members of the community, which may be capitalised upon.

Producing a checklist of requirements

By this is meant a list of requirements for implementing policy. Various items will be repetitive of the checklist for producing a policy document. The checklist should include:

- overall rationale for including these curriculum areas in the school's overall programme;
- aims, objectives, content;
- time allocations;
- approach to whole-school organisation of these areas;
- staff responsibilities;

- resource requirements and accessibility;
- monitoring, assessment and recording techniques.

Clarifying content and objectives

This will include helping all staff to understand and appreciate the subject area content and objectives of geography and environmental education, and the structure of these areas of learning as set out in Chapter 2. Both lead to the development of knowledge, understanding, skills and values. A successful policy document may give examples of these components, such as:

Knowledge	of places, of people's homes, of food ingredients, of measuring the weather, of types of farm, of landscape features.
Understanding	of links between local and distant places, of ways in which people can harm or destroy parts of the natural world, of the need to manage or protect aspects of our environment.
Skills	of observation, communication, problem-solving decision-making; of being able to understand issues from the points of view of other people.
Values	having respect for the natural and built environments; having a sense of personal concern for the care of the planet or features within it.

Providing a rationale for teaching and learning methods

Content and objectives, once defined, have implications for teaching and learning methods. The need for emphasis on first-hand, investigatory learning experiences has already been stressed. Successful implementation of policy will no doubt involve the application of this, plus a range of other approaches to teaching and learning. These may include structured input (from the teacher or secondary resources such as books, computer programs, videos), individual research, role plays, group discussions/debate and experiential activities. The rationale statement may emphasise:

- that as geographical and environmental issues are multifaceted and complex, investigatory and co-operative learning is likely to be more successful than competitive learning;
- that relevant skills underpin the acquisition of knowledge and understanding of geographical concepts;
- that the ethos of the school itself cannot be separated from the content of geographical and environmental education. Does the school environment reflect care and concern? What messages are implicit in the way

the school and its grounds are maintained? Does the school community reflect qualities of co-operation, tolerance, respect and empathy?

Establishing mechanisms for evaluation, review and development

By this we mean evaluation, review and development of the whole-school policy. As the delivery of geography and environmental education is a school-wide matter, it is not sufficient merely to collect data about, assess and record individual pupils' achievements and progress. Overall management, rationale, teaching approaches and the ways in which the whole-school environment has been developed must also be subject to regular review. Once again, it is inappropriate to prescribe a complete set of evaluation and review questions, as individual circumstances should build these into a policy statement. Examples may include:

- Who was involved in working out and writing the school policy and its goals?
- How was the policy communicated to all parties concerned?
- What programme content was included?
- How were individual schemes and programmes evaluated?
- Has an inventory of resources (including human and community resources) been made and kept up to date?
- Has the whole-school environment been developed and managed to its full potential for geographical work?
- What future action is planned or needed?

Some final comments on the evaluation and review of school-wide programmes focus attention on the effectiveness of individual schemes or topics, which may have been followed by one or more classes. The curriculum co-ordinator may find the following questions helpful when carrying out or discussing a review of a completed topic:

- Was the topic/scheme based on practical involvement and the pupils' first-hand experiences of the environment? Was the acquisition of geographical skills a starting point or an integral feature of the work done?
- Did the topic/scheme have clear aims, stated both in a conceptual underpinning (e.g. the pupils investigated change through the year on the local farm) and in a plan of content which included knowledge and understanding from other key curriculum areas?
- Did the topic/scheme identify only those other areas of the curriculum with which useful and meaningful links for integration could be achieved? Did it avoid trying to incorporate every conceivable subject area merely for 'the sake of it'? In other words, did geographical education provide a discernible core of work?
- Did teacher observations and examples of children's writing and other

recordings provide an ongoing component of record-keeping and assessment throughout the year?

- Was a wide variety of teaching methods used, including teacher-led discussions and presentations, whole-class activities, and group and individual investigations?
- Was due regard paid to the development of skills, including a wide range of cross-curricular skills (e.g. observation, problem-solving, communication)?
- Were elements of the formal National Curriculum entitlement at the forefront of planning? For example, did planning take account of progression from local to global issues? Were attitudes, values and beliefs recognised as key elements of the learning process? Did content directly relate to National Curriculum guidelines?

ASSESSMENT AND RECORD-KEEPING

If a school policy and individual schemes of work are to be implemented successfully, appropriate arrangements for assessment and record-keeping must be in place. In the case of the National Curriculum for schools in England, specific assessment suggestions for geography Key Stage 1 are defined and published. These aim to provide information on pupils' achievements and progress in learning. Assessment thus relates to subject-specific content.

Progress in the theme of environmental education, however, can only be achieved and recorded through planned programmes of study which are devised and monitored to take account of the cross-curricular nature of learning. In other words, environmental education should be included in the progressive schemes of work of other subject areas. This is interpreted to mean cross-referencing with the attainment targets and statements of attainment of the core and foundation subjects. Assessment should relate to the three central teaching objectives for environmental education, i.e. knowledge and understanding, skills and concepts. Thus the national framework for assessment will be an essential baseline since a great deal of environmental teaching and learning will occur through teaching of the core and foundation subjects. That aside, innovatory or original school-devised methods of environmental assessment are necessary in relation to its other various elements, notably the development of attitudes and concerns. Assessment in this area should take account of tasks which help pupils to learn *about* the environment, tasks which involve learning in or *through* the environment, and tasks which involve learning *for* the environment.

For the purpose of this volume, attention is focused on methods of collecting and recording assessment information, which are clearly transferable to a focus either on geographical or environmental content. Precise documentation and methods of recording will inevitably vary from school to school, reflecting individual needs and circumstances. Pupil records, which provide a profile of geographical education and related environmental experiences and attainments across the curriculum, need to be maintained by the class teacher or subject co-ordinator. Complete documentation may comprise a wide range of written material, including pupil profile sheets, class and individual records, samples of children's work, overall schemes and specific learning plans.

Success in the collection of relevant assessment information is dependent upon crucial teacher skills, notably observing, listening, testing (in the formal or informal sense), interacting with pupils (conversation, questions and feedback), and scrutinising recorded outcomes of learning tasks. The essence of assessment in geography is thus communication between teacher and learner – communication which helps the learner to appreciate what has been learned, and the teacher to plan tasks and first-hand experiences that will promote future learning of concepts and skills or development of attitudes/concern. In early years classrooms this will necessarily involve time for watching, listening and questioning individual pupils and groups as well as interpretation of children's work.

Attention is now focused on the teacher skills of observation, listening and questioning, which are of critical importance to geographical education because of its emphasis on experiential and investigatory learning.

Observation should be approached as a skilled and strategic task, given that classroom observations may either be planned or spontaneous. Spontaneous observations are an important aspect of all classroom situations, perhaps particularly so when pupils go about their learning tasks in an independent way, knowing what their investigations involve and the availability of the resources necessary to perform them. Obviously no teacher can possibly record what is happening in a classroom all the time. It is far better to focus on specific features or interactions, and to record significant events in a variety of contexts than to watch a class without a focus. Suitable contexts may include:

- Individual tasks, e.g. selecting appropriate equipment to measure a desk, drawing a simple plan or map.
- Group work, e.g. building a model village according to a predetermined plan, involving the collecting together of the necessary elements of the model, discussion, allocating tasks, listening to the views of others and collaborating to produce results.

A cautionary note about spontaneous observations is that early years teachers generally have 'eyes in the back of their heads' and a tremendous capacity to notice many events all at the same time. This in many respects is a great asset – but can be a weakness in assessment. Partial information may be acquired in this way, which may be inadequate for making judgements on learning. Whenever possible, spontaneous observations should be recorded carefully to 'back up' or assist the planned schedules.

Planned observations will have a clear objective; for example, to assess whether a pupil understands that a knowledge of direction can help in the location of objects in space or whether he or she can successfully reduce a 30cm line to the scale of a half. Such observations and their results will be informative and help with future planning, confirming progress made in teaching and learning. When planning observations, it is necessary to decide exactly what will be looked for, ways in which it will be tested or checked, and whether the task will involve interaction with the learner or simply seeing what is taking place. Decisions must also be made about whether the interchange will be used to extend the learner's thinking at that time, and how the outcomes of the observations will be recorded.

Checklist for planned observations

- Decide what/who you are going to observe and why.
- Decide whether you intend to test or check the observation in another way or at another time.
- Decide whether you will be unobtrusive or whether you wish to interact with the teaching during the observation process.
- Arrange the individual group or class so that the observations can take place in a 'natural' way (without abnormal behaviour or complete rearrangement of furniture).
- Concentrate on the task in hand.
- Take detailed notes of what you see – perhaps recorded on a pre-planned form (Figure 5.2).
- Make time to read and interpret notes while the observations are fresh in the mind.
- Decide how they will relate to other assessment data.
- Decide how results will assist overall assessment procedures and the design of further appropriate learning tasks.

Figure 5.2 provides a suggested design for a planned observation recording sheet.

Listening is such a crucial skill in the assessment process that perhaps a separate recording sheet should be designed and filled in at appropriate times. Comments made above about observations also apply to listening strategies. Many early years teachers are outstandingly good at listening to six conversations at once and extracting their essence, but is this enough to illuminate children's learning? Sessions for listening need careful planning if results are to be valid and useful. Some sessions may involve a teacher in listening while all children are busily engaged in tasks. At other times, children and teacher may listen together; for example, when an individual

Name(s) of pupils observed		
Year group	Date of observation	Time

Ongoing work relating to geographical attainment targets (✓)

AT1 ☐   AT2 ☐   AT3 ☐   AT4 ☐   AT5 ☐   and/or

Education for ☐   from ☐   about ☐   the environment

Specific task(s) observed

What happened

Specific difficulties encountered by pupil(s)

Any further comments/recommendations

Related assessment details	Observer

Figure 5.2   Recording observations: suggested format
Note: Figures 5.2 and 5.3 are designed to take account of the Attainment Target Structure of the original National Curriculum Order for geography, but can be adapted to any curriculum content

is reading a story out loud or the class is having a discussion. Matters to consider when planning listening include:

- Decide what/who the focus of attention will be. Is it to be on what the children say to each other or to you?
- Decide whether you intend to test or check outcomes by asking pupils to repeat what they have said or explain it further.
- Decide whether you will be unobtrusive, or whether you wish to engage in conversation while also listening.
- Arrange the pupil(s) in such a way that listening can take place 'naturally'.
- Take notes of what you hear – perhaps recorded on a pre-planned form such as Figure 5.3.
- Decide how these will relate to other assessment data.
- Decide whether you wish to talk more (or hear more) about the conversation you have recorded.
- Decide how results will assist overall assessment procedures and the design of further appropriate learning tasks.

Figure 5.3 provides a suggested design for a planned listening recording sheet.

The use of a tape recorder can be valuable, particularly where several children are engaged in discussion and it is difficult to take adequate notes. Be aware, however, that tape recorders pick up unwelcome background noise, and that tapes take a long time to listen to, and even longer to transcribe.

The skills of questioning play a crucial role in the assessment process, alongside observation, listening and testing. The range and quality of questions posed by a teacher will reveal not only ways in which the learner is thinking, but also the kind of thinking being encouraged and expected. Thus questioning results in important two-way communication in the learning process.

Questions can be posed at a variety of levels, ranging from simple 'closed' questions of fact, requiring little more than 'yes' or 'no' answers, through to sophisticated questions of analysis, synthesis and evaluation, such as 'What do you think would happen if. . .?', 'Can you think of ways in which . . .?'

Each category of question produces a response that initiates a specific kind of thought process. By employing questions at a variety of levels or categories, learners will engage in a variety of cognitive processes. Lower-order thinking involves retrieval of facts or information from memory. Questions involving thinking of this kind often begin with the words: What? Where? When? Who? The knowledge recalled will probably be in the same form as it was learnt and will not go beyond that basic information with which the learner is familiar. Higher-order thinking requires a change

Name(s) of pupils observed		
Year group	Date of observation	Time

Ongoing work relating to geographical attainment targets (✓)

AT1 ☐   AT2 ☐   AT3 ☐   AT4 ☐   AT5 ☐   and/or

Education for ☐   from ☐   about ☐   the environment

Specific task(s) pupil(s) engaged in

What was said	Who said it

Notes on responses/difficulties made apparent

Any further comments/recommendations	Was the conversation recorded? ☐ Yes ☐ No
Related assessment details	Recorder

Figure 5.3   Recording listening: suggested format

in the form of existing knowledge, perhaps to compare or contrast, to apply it or extend it, explain or analyse, reorganise or evaluate, synthesise or solve problems. In other words, learned material must be recalled and then used or applied to provide an outcome or answer of a higher cognitive level. Both levels of questioning are essential for effective progression in geographical education. Lower-order questioning will encourage memorisation of facts and rote learning; higher-order questioning is essential for promoting more complex thinking processes associated with issues and the promotion of concern for the world.

Figure 5.4 gives examples of questions in various categories, and the required thinking related to them, derived from appropriate elements of curriculum content. Readers are encouraged to interpret their own class-room and fieldwork situations in a similar way, thus providing analysis of children's thinking which could contribute to an overall profile of assess-ment in geography. Figure 5.5 provides a sample recording sheet for this purpose. The middle and right-hand columns are left blank so that the sheet can be filled in for an individual child. The right-hand column should be used to record examples of answers provided by the pupil alongside the questions asked by the teacher at the appropriate level of required thinking; that is, the sheet is used to record responses to planned questions posed by the teacher. It provides an 'at a glance' guide to the level of questioning that a pupil is capable of responding to in a consistent and successful way. Questioning should not be left to chance. The effective teacher will plan for questioning in geography with the same rigour as for any other aspect of the early years reaching role.

In summary, the use of questioning alongside observation and listening helps a teacher to ascertain:

- whether the pupil has learned the intended outcomes of specific tasks and activities;
- the success (or failure) of specific teaching strategies;
- how the pupil is performing relative to others of a similar age;
- whether the pupil is ready for the next stage in a particular progression of learning;
- the nature of particular difficulties (if any) that the pupil is experiencing.

Together with testing (formal and informal) and interpretation of pupils' written work, these skills form the basis for successful recording and assessment procedures, and make a substantial contribution to planning and evaluation of tasks, schemes and programmes of work in geographical education.

Checklist of records for teaching and learning

Figure 5.6 provides a checklist of the kinds of record that a school should

Category	Teacher question	Response
Knowledge	Recall of facts and basic understandings or observations	1 How wide was the playground? 2 What is the name of the river we saw? 3 What animals does the farmer have?
Comprehension	Comparing, contrasting, describing, explaining	1 Can you explain why farmers grow food? 2 Which is higher – the river bank or the house on the hillside?
Application	Applying knowledge to solve problems, classifying, selecting, using	1 Can you follow this plan to put the model village back in the right place? 2 Do all the world's people live in houses like ours?
Analysis	Drawing conclusions, making inferences, finding causes, determining and using evidence	1 Why do you think people in the Arctic eat a lot of fish? 2 Why is water running down the side of the hill?
Synthesis	Solving problems, making predictions, proposing	What do you think would happen if the world got warmer and all the snow melted?
Evaluation	Judging, evaluating, deciding, appraising	Do you think it is a good idea to cut down trees in rain forests?

Figure 5.4 Summary of teacher's questions and cognitive processes related to Key Stage 1 geography

keep for geographical and environmental work, including formal and informal assessment details.

Chapter 6 contains several examples of activities suitable for staff discussion and inset sessions which focus on assessment tasks.

Name of pupil		
Topic		
Category	Teacher question	Response
Knowledge		
Comprehension		
Application		
Analysis		
Synthesis		
Evaluation		

Figure 5.5   Questioning: individual recording sheet

Record sheets

Schools are already snowed under with charts, ticklists, SAT booklets and tables to fill in, and countless hours will have been spent in every staffroom discussing the merits and drawbacks of checklists and profile sheets. The writer has no wish to add to the proliferation of simple recording sheets available. It is assumed that staff are well used to filling in written records relating to National Curriculum attainment. A focus has therefore been placed on the augmentation of records by teacher assessment skills, which can make a significant contribution to individual children's profiles.

The chapter does, however, conclude with suggestions for recording the acquisition of concepts, skills and attitudes in environmental work since this is less likely to be covered by standard record sheets suitable for the core and foundation subjects.

Figure 5.7 provides a way of recording the main concepts which any topic of a geographical or environmental nature has focused upon. To begin with, the teacher merely brainstorms, or lists the main concepts covered.

TEACHER RECORDS	CHILD RECORDS
Relating to past work Geographical topics completed Ticklists of ATs covered both in geography and related areas Aspects of programmes of study covered	**Relating to past work** Portfolio of work samples SAT results Details of achievement derived from other sources, e.g. teacher observations, recordings
Relating to future work Forecast of future topics Lesson details – with plans of ATs to be covered	**Relating to future work** Comments on the child's profile in terms of next appropriate stages of learning Identification of remedial work if necessary

Figure 5.6   Checklist for record-keeping

Purpose

Class _____ **Dates of topic** _____

Topic title

List of concepts important in work covered

_____

_____

_____

_____

_____

Analysis of the above to show the five key concepts covered, in rank order of significance

1 _____

2 _____

3 _____

4 _____

5 _____

Figure 5.7 Recording concepts in environmental geography

He or she is then asked to name the five priority concepts in rank order of importance. This will be of help when considering whether individual children have mastered the concepts deemed to be of significance.

Figure 5.8 gives an outline for a recording sheet which can be used to show the level of mastery of the significant concepts by individual children. It also provides scope for reflecting on the development of skills and attitudes in environmental education. The headings at the top of each of the last four columns are suggestions only. No doubt individual schools will design appropriate wording for heading up the specific skills under

Name	Understanding of five key concepts	Communication skills: relating to others	Ability to raise questions, solve problems	Awareness of issues	Demonstration of personal responsibility/concern

Fill in by ticking boxes relating to understanding of concepts: (the five key concepts identified)

✓✓✓ high level of understanding
✓✓ some understanding
✓ little understanding

Other boxes can be filled in by ticks, or preferably by writing three or four key words

Figure 5.8   Recording progress in environmental education: concepts, skills, attitudes

scrutiny, and the development of positive attitudes and concern for environmental issues.

Children's recording

Last but not least, no chapter on record-keeping and assessment would be complete without reference to sheets suitable for children to make their own recordings when undertaking first-hand investigatory work or field studies.

Figures 5.9 and 5.10 are suggestions for sheets suitable for recording children's experiences and feelings while undertaking tasks in environmental geography.

What do you think of the street? Place a tick in one of the boxes below:

I think the High Street is:

Beautiful	☐	☐	Ugly
Quiet	☐	☐	Noisy
Tidy	☐	☐	Untidy
Deserted	☐	☐	Crowded
Open	☐	☐	Cramped
Safe	☐	☐	Dangerous
Windy	☐	☐	Calm
Warm	☐	☐	Cold
Exciting	☐	☐	Boring
Good for old people	☐	☐	Bad for old people
Old	☐	☐	New
Dirty	☐	☐	Clean
Friendly	☐	☐	Unfriendly
Good for children	☐	☐	Bad for children
Sleepy	☐	☐	Lively

Figure 5.9   Thinking about the street

Where did you go?	What were you reminded of?
	What was your funniest thought?
	What was your strangest thought?

| What did you taste? | What did you smell? |

| What did you hear? | What did you feel |

| ? | What words did you encounter? (spoken, written) |

| What did you see? (graphic answers only) |

Figure 5.10   Questions to ask on a trail

Chapter 6

Activities for school-based in-service development meetings

INTRODUCTION

This chapter outlines a number of activities which could be adopted for staff discussion meetings or more formal in-service training sessions. They are appropriate for use by a gathering the size of an average school staff. Each is freestanding, and aims to enhance thinking or practice on some aspect of geographical education or environmental geography. Thus the activities are not in any particular order, nor are they intended to follow on from each other in a planned sequence. They are intended to be thought-provoking, useful, relevant to every staff member, and indeed fun to take part in. They aim to provide practical reflection on a number of theoretical issues raised in this book.

ACTIVITY 1 BACK FROM THE HOLIDAYS

Aims and organisation

This activity is designed to help staff reflect upon their own travels, their potential for contributing to geographical education in the school, and on the accuracy of knowledge gleaned in this way. It is ideal for an autumn term 'one-off' staff meeting, when summer holidays are fresh in people's minds. You will need a large empty notice board, some paper, felt pens and drawing pins. Ask each staff member to bring along one photograph or poster relating to his or her holiday travels – of a location abroad or in the UK.

Procedure

Go round the assembled staff and ask each person to put up his or her chosen photograph on the board and talk for a few moments about the place visited – the things they enjoyed best about it, anything they did not enjoy, and to comment on perceived differences between this place and the home area. At the end of each short talk, let other members of the staff jot down questions or comments on a piece of paper (one can be scribe for the group); for example, anything they particularly wanted to know about the place that the speaker didn't mention, anything they can add to what the speaker mentioned because of their own personal knowledge, anything they disagree with. Pin the sheets by the photographs, and discuss the results. They should provide information on the collective knowledge of the staff, which should be helpful in selecting places for study in future topics; give an idea of photographs and other resources available about places visited; and, above all, give insight into teachers' own gaps in knowledge or even stereotypical knowledge about places gained as a result of reading or a brief visit to a destination. This overview should be helpful when developing topics that provide accurate, up-to-date information about distant lands, and help to raise awareness of possible pitfalls to be subsequently avoided in the classroom. End the session by making lists of available resources, including objects and artefacts from the places discussed.

ACTIVITY 2   REFINING A TOPIC WEB

Aims and organisation

This activity may well be familiar to many schools, but it is included to emphasise the need for planned refining of topic webs. These frequently do not go beyond a brainstorming session in any systematic way at whole-school level. You will need several large (poster-size) sheets of paper and felt pens.

Procedure

Decide on the geographical topic to be planned and elect a scribe for the occasion. Construct a topic web through a brainstorming session:

- Write the topic title in the centre of a large sheet of paper.
- Invite staff members to call out possible activities, thoughts and ideas relating to the topic as quickly as possible. The scribe should write these around the topic title, in no particular order or sequence.
- Photocopy the end product, and give a copy to smaller teams (e.g. two members of staff or even an individual) representing specific subject areas. Make sure that teams cover each core and foundation subject and cross-curricular themes.

Each sub-team should then refine the web by identifying the activities and suggestions which can be linked in a meaningful way to the subject area being considered. Geography should, of course, be considered by a sub-team, even though it is the focus of the whole topic.

Reassemble as a whole staff and redraw a refined web with the topic title in the centre, surrounded by subject-headed listings provided by the sub-teams. It could well be that some subjects dominate the web, while others have little documentation. This is a healthy state of affairs, reinforcing a key principle of good topic work which is that some areas link meaningfully through certain topics, and no topic should 'drag in every subject' for the sake of it. Acknowledge the key areas linking with geography on this particular occasion, and make notes for future reference of areas not covered or marginally related, so that these may warrant attention by other means or at other times.

Reconvene the sub-teams and let each now add specifics of attainment targets that may be covered for their area (if relevant) and a breakdown of the suggested activities into those which aim to teach skills, those aimed at developing concepts, and those which promote learning of values and attitudes. Feed this information back for incorporation on to the master plan.

Figure 6.1 provides a diagrammatic representation of the stages involved in topic refining.

ACTIVITY 3   AN EAR FOR GEOGRAPHY

Aims and organisation

This activity aims to give practice in developing the skills of listening in order to review, monitor and assess children's geographical learning. Throughout this book it has been emphasised that oral work in the first three years in school is of the utmost importance; therefore, a teacher's listening skills are critical. Prepare for this session by asking one teacher from each year group (Reception, Y1, Y2) to make a short tape recording of a pair of children or small group undertaking tasks in geography, and perhaps interacting with the teacher while performing their allocated tasks. (This itself is a skill worthy of practice, as discussed in Chapter 5.)

Procedure

Listen to the tapes, either as a whole staff or in groups (i.e. exchange each other's) and discuss them. Consider evidence of learning or understanding relating to any of the attainment targets for geography (or areas of learning in environmental education) and any obvious gaps or mistakes in the children's learning. Consider the role of the teacher, if applicable, as heard on the recording. People's interpretation of the recordings could be written on sheets designed for the purpose, such as the pro forma for listening suggested in Chapter 5 (see Figure 5.3). No attempt should be made to transcribe the tapes, as this is a time-consuming task which cannot be done

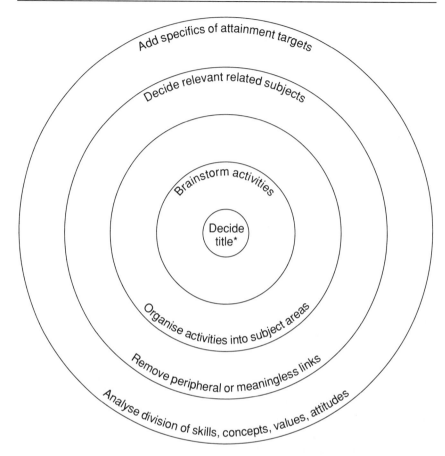

Add specifics of attainment targets

Decide relevant related subjects

Brainstorm activities

Decide title*

Organise activities into subject areas

Remove peripheral or meaningless links

Analyse division of skills, concepts, values, attitudes

* The decision should be based on the application of organised criteria rather than 'pulling it out of thin air'.

Figure 6.1   The stages involved in topic refining

as a matter of routine when assessing children's geographical work. Discuss the place of recorded evidence in your overall school plans for assessment of geographical learning.

ACTIVITY 4   LOCAL TO GLOBAL

Aims and organisation

The purpose of this activity is to help staff consider whether a good balance has been achieved in geographical and environmental education between local work and work on more distant environments, and between the

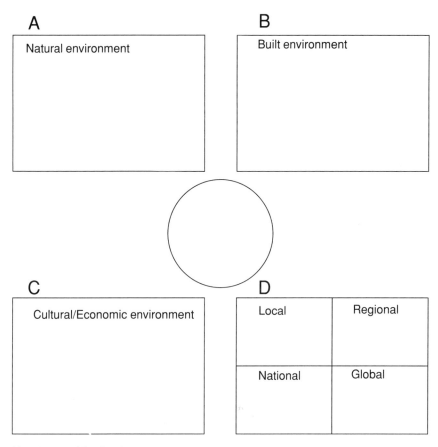

A

Natural environment

B

Built environment

C

Cultural/Economic environment

D

| Local | Regional |
| National | Global |

How to use this sheet

- Write the topic title in the centre circle
- Place ticks as follows in boxes A, B and C to indicate emphasis.

    ✓ ✓ ✓ ✓ major emphasis
    ✓ ✓ ✓   some emphasis
    ✓ ✓   little emphasis
    ✗   no emphasis

- Place one or more ticks in the appropriate sections of box D to show the emphasis of the study in terms of geographical location(s).

Figure 6.2   Recording sheet: local to global coverage

various aspects of the environment that can be focused upon (natural, built, cultural/economic). Throughout the first three years in school, all children should pursue topics and tasks which cover this range. Staff will need copies of schemes of work or topic plans for the academic year (applicable to all three years) and copies of a recording sheet based on Figure 6.2.

Procedure

Divide the staff into groups, and ask each group to analyse the content of one particular topic to be taught during the year. Between them the staff should cover all the topics to be undertaken throughout the school. Analysis should result in the filling-in of a sheet for each topic, based on Figure 6.2.

Reconvene as a whole staff, and study the sheets as a complete set. Consider the questions:

- Is there a balance among local, regional, national and global studies throughout the school?
- Is there an increasing emphasis on global studies in topics designed for older pupils?
- Do the planned topics allow for every child to study aspects of the natural, built and cultural/economic environments in each year of schooling?

This analysis should lead to refining or possible restructuring of topics in order to achieve the best possible breadth and balance across the various dimensions.

ACTIVITY 5   ANALYSING CHILDREN'S WORK

Aims and organisation

This activity stimulates discussion on examples of children's written work in geography, and leads to some understanding of difficulties involved in using children's work for assessment purposes. It should reveal the extent to which there is agreement among staff about children's levels of performance, as indicated by their writing and drawings. You will need the examples of work provided below in Figures 6.3, 6.4, 6.5 and 6.6.

Procedures

The examples of work provided deliberately do not indicate the ages of the children responsible for them. Neither do they suggest whether they are

a plah oF our table

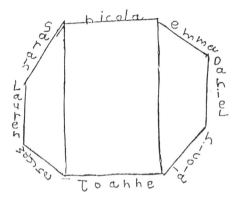

Figure 6.3 Example (a) of children's work which might be used for assessment purposes

'good', 'poor' or 'average' in terms of performance at any given level of attainment. Suggest that the staff study them carefully, bearing in mind the attainment targets and levels of attainment for geography, and try to write a set of criteria which could be used when making judgements about levels at which the children are working. Differences in opinion will be inevitable. These can be discussed and attempts made to reconcile them as far as possible so that a consensus of opinion is arrived at which will be helpful when looking at future examples of work.

A follow-up activity could involve staff undertaking to provide examples of work from their own classrooms, selected because they meet the agreed criteria for the various levels of attainment. These new examples can then be shared with the staff as a whole, and further discussion can ensue about the application of assessment criteria.

ACTIVITY 6 GEOGRAPHY THROUGH STORY

Aims and organisation

This activity aims to give practice in the analysis and development of the potential for geographical education in children's stories. It is based on case

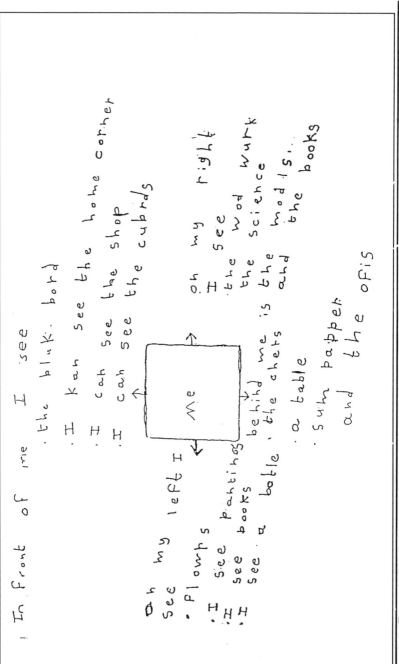

i In front of me I see
  ·the bluk. bord)
 ·I kan see the home corner
  ·I can see the shop
  ·I can see the cubrds

Oh my left I
see · Flowrhs
·I see pantings behind
·I see books me is the chers
·I see a table · a table
            ·shm papper
            · and the ofis

oh my right
I see the wod wurk
the science
and the modls...
the books

Figure 6.4 Example (b) of children's work which might be used for assessment purposes

This is where we sit in red group

Figure 6.5   Example (c) of children's work which might be used for assessment
purposes

study 5, The use of story, in Chapter 4. One or more story books considered
to have geographical potential will be required for this activity, perhaps
selected from the list provided on pages 171–4. The number of stories
required will clearly depend on the number of staff at the meeting, but it is
suggested that groups of two to three people analyse one story.

Procedure

Divide staff into groups of two or three. Set aside half an hour for them to
read, discuss and analyse a chosen story for its geographical potential.
Record results of deliberations in written form as in the analysis of *Red Fox*
given on pages 121–4. Suggestions should refer to both the text and the
illustrations in terms of their potential for developing geographical vocabulary and linking with attainment targets.

   Reconvene as a whole staff group and discuss the potential of all the
stories analysed. Type up suggestions, and agree to trial them in classrooms, leading to the production of written evaluations.

   At a subsequent staff meeting, circulate and consider each of the evalu-

Figure 6.6 Example (d) of children's work which might be used for assessment purposes

ations. Make decisions on the appropriateness and potential of the trialled stories. File the assessments of potential together with evaluations, comments and perhaps examples of children's work deriving from the stories in your collection of school resources.

Chapter 7

Resources

BEATING THE BUDGET

Successful teaching and learning in geography are inevitably dependent to a greater or lesser extent on resources; and with current and ever-increasing pressures on schools' budgets the acquisition of a wide range of useful items is no doubt a daunting, if not impossible, challenge.

This chapter begins, therefore, with some general comments on and advice aimed at reducing levels of anxiety in school budget holders, generated by the prospect of having to do conjuring tricks with cash before any worthwhile geographical education can be achieved.

In the first instance, schools may be surprised at the wide range of relevant materials that can be used from resource banks of other subject areas. Many general reading books, for example, commonly found in early years classrooms, are ideal for developing into geographical topics or for illustrating specific concepts and issues – more will be said about this later in the chapter. Many items purchased for science education are obviously transferable to geographical studies, notably equipment for collecting, observing and magnifying, and for studying the weather. Sand and water apparatus is highly relevant for investigatory studies and experimentation in various aspects of physical geography. Mathematics equipment, in the form of measuring devices, and material for reinforcing elements of size and shape, is necessary for many tasks relating to the teaching of geographical skills, and resources of technology and information technology are clearly important across the geography curriculum. It would probably be true to say that every infant school could ask its pupils to undertake a sophisticated range of geographical tasks without purchase of specialist equipment.

Furthermore, an impressive bank of resources for geography can be built up at little or no cost apart from effort on the part of staff – and all schools are encouraged to begin establishing such a bank now, if a collection is not already in place. For example:

- Make a school collection of maps of various scales, sizes and uses; consult the local Tourist Information Centre and travel agent, look out for maps in papers and magazines, and try to acquire a range of published maps, e.g. an Ordnance Survey map of the local area, a world map, an A–Z. Visit the local planning office, and ask whether any maps are available; the local studies section of the library may also be helpful.

- Make collections of objects/illustrative material from distant places. When abroad, or in distant parts of the UK, seek out photographs, posters, examples of local craft work, tapes of authentic music, items or pictures of national dress, details of special festivals, customs and traditional foods. Sketch or photograph homes and people.

  Suggest that every member of staff does this when going out and about or on holiday. Soon a large collection of objects relating to places will be assembled at comparatively little expense.

- Make a photograph bank. As with the above suggestion, each member of staff could be asked to add to a central collection after a holiday or visit away from the local area. One person could undertake to go out with a camera into the neighbourhood and make a specific collection of photographs of the locality. These could become useful for history topics in the future, as features of the local area inevitably change over time.

- Make a collection of interesting cuttings of geographical interest from local newspapers. This has the same potential as a photograph bank in terms of a future source of information about change.

Here is a checklist of general resources for geography and environmental work. This should be helpful to curriculum co-ordinators who are trying to build up a range of items to service teaching and learning. Some cost money, others are free and could well augment the budget-beating ideas set out above.

GENERAL CHECKLIST OF RESOURCES

People   Make a list of staff and contacts who have visited distant lands or lived in other places in the UK and who would be prepared to come and talk about them.

Make a list of people in the local community, perhaps elderly people, who could talk about aspects of life which have changed, or specialist workers (policeman, shopkeeper, vicar) who are knowledgeable about specific local buildings, places or jobs.

Keep these lists in 'file form' in a central place, so that staff can add to them, and the curriculum co-ordinator can check and update them regularly.

Places   Make an inventory of places (in the locality and further afield) of particular geographical interest for fieldwork, with a note of opening hours/special features if appropriate. Again, this should be kept centrally so that it can be updated.

Maintain an associated box file, containing literature/brochures relating to the places.

Maps   Collect as wide a range of maps as possible. Also, acquire globes, atlases and air photographs. Local newspaper offices often have air photographs. Local studies sections of libraries usually have maps and photographs which can be copied; so too have planning offices. Ordnance Survey maps are an important aspect of the collection, and details about acquiring these are given below.

Books and   Reference books about themes/topics, e.g. food, homes;
written   also about distant places, world issues, festivals and
sources   customs. Newspaper cuttings, tourist brochures, leaflets, wallcharts. Stories set in distant places or about journeys. Recipe books from around the world, written sources about the local area (from the library, the planning office, etc.).

Note that a school collection of books and other forms of written material should promote accurate knowledge about our multicultural world, and avoid images of stereotyping and bias.

Illustrative   Photographs, posters, slides, filmstrips. Travel agents are
material   often a useful source. The same cautionary note about accuracy as given for written sources obviously applies to illustrations. Try to keep a balance between familiar and unfamiliar people and environments.

Music   Collect tape recordings/records of music from distant places, pictures or examples of traditional musical instruments.

Mechanical   Microcomputers and software, cameras, television programmes, radio programmes, videos of distant lands, films.

Tape recordings of current events or of people talking about their lives, their past, their jobs, etc.

Miscellaneous   Special equipment, e.g. for weather recording, pond dipping, soil studies, working out direction.

Models, e.g. landscape models, stream channels.

Objects, e.g. examples of clothing, craft work from distant places, menus from foreign restaurants.

Many of the above items will need careful selection, in order to strike an appropriate balance between items applicable to the various elements of content and authenticity and accuracy of knowledge. The task of the school co-ordinator will be to encourage the collection of, check and maintain up-to-date resources; also to help the rest of the staff make the distinction between that which is teacher resource material for study and appropriate interpretation, and that which is appropriate for the pupils themselves to use. Both have a place in the school collection and, as with all resources, staff will need to discuss and make decisions about how both children and staff access geographical materials so that an equitable arrangement benefits the school as a whole.

The remainder of this chapter is devoted to providing specific help and suggestions for resourcing geographical work in the early years.

STORY BOOKS SUITABLE AS STARTING POINTS IN GEOGRAPHY

Rosie's Walk, Pat Hutchins, Bodley Head
Billy Goats Gruff, Fran Hunia, Ladybird
Robin Hood, Joan Collins, Ladybird
Three Little Pigs, Fran Hunia, Ladybird
Goldilocks and the Three Bears, Fran Hunia, Ladybird
Little Red Riding Hood, Tony Ross, Penguin
The Lighthouse Keeper's Lunch, Ronda and David Armitage, Penguin
The Enormous Crocodile, Roald Dahl, Penguin
Don't Forget the Bacon, Pat Hutchins, Bodley Head
Postman Pat's Letters on Ice, John Cunliffe, Hippo Books
Topsy and Tim – Snowy Day, Jean and Gareth Adamson, Blackie
Let's Go to Sally's Place, Pat Edwards, Longman
Crafty Chameleon, Mwenye Hadithi, Hodder & Stoughton
Have You Seen Stanley?, Pat Edwards, Longman
Alfi Gets in First, Shirley Hughes, Bodley Head
Scragg's Flowers, Malcolm Yorke, Arnold-Wheaton
I'll Take You to Mrs Cole, Nigel Gray and Michael Foreman, Macmillan
My School, Sumiko, Heinemann
What-A-Mess, Frank Muir, A. & C. Black
There's No Such Thing as a Dragon, Jack Kent, Blackie
The Lion and Albert, Marriott Edgar, Methuen
Burglar Bill, Allan and Janet Ahlberg, Heinemann
Goodnight, Goodnight, Eve Rice, Penguin
Cops and Robbers, Allan and Janet Ahlberg, Heinemann
The Fox Went Out On a Chilly Night, Peter Spier, Penguin
The Tail of the Mouse, Joan M. Lexau, Ginn
On the Way Home, Jill Murphy, Macmillan
Dear Daddy, Philippe Dupasquier, Penguin

The Joggers, Pat Edwards, Longman
Just Awful, Alma Marshak Whitney, Armada
Weather, Jan Pienkowski, Heinemann
Can't Catch Me, John Prater, Penguin
Where the Wild Things Are, Maurice Sendak, Bodley Head
One World, Michael Foreman, Andersen Press
When Dad Cuts Down the Chestnut Tree, Pam Ayres, Walker Books
A Balloon for Grandad, Nigel Gray and Jane Ray, Collins
When Dad Fills in the Garden Pond, Pam Ayres, Walker Books
The World That Jack Built, Ruth Brown, Andersen Press
Ladybird, Ladybird, Ruth Brown, Beaver Books
The Twins in Greece/in France, Sally Kilroy, Orchard Books
Stories From Our Street, Richard Tulloch, Cambridge University Press
A Country Faraway, Nigel Gray and Philippe Dupasquier, Andersen Press
Where the Forest Meets the Sea, Jeannie Baker, Walker Books
A Garden in the City, Gerda Muller, Macdonald
Dinosaurs and All That Rubbish, Michael Foreman, Penguin
Will It Rain Today?, Althea, Dinosaur Publications
Lucy's Year, Stephen Weatherill, Two-Can Publishing
It's Mine, Leo Lionni, Hodder & Stoughton
Have You Seen Birds?, Joanne Oppenheim, Hippo
Deep in the Wood, Richard Bell, Little Mammoth
Oi, Get Off Our Train, John Burningham, Random Century
Tusk, Tusk, David McKee, Andersen Press
The Elephant and the Bad Baby, Elfrida Vipont, Penguin
How Can an Elephant Hide?, David McPhail, Methuen
Oxford Reading Tree   The Dump, Roderick Hunt, Oxford University Press
   A Day in London, Roderick Hunt, Oxford University Press
   The Flying Carpet, Roderick Hunt, Oxford University Press
   The Emergency, Mike Poulton, Oxford University Press
The Journey Home, Joanne Flindall, Walker Books
In a Dark, Dark Wood, June Melser and Joy Cowley, Arnold-Wheaton
Four Fat Rats, Cathy Bellows, Macmillan
The Jolly Witch, Dick King-Smith, Simon & Schuster
The Invitation, Nicola Smee, Collins
Lost, David McPhail, Little, Brown and Co
Once Upon a Time, Gwenda Turner, Penguin
How Stories Came into the World, Joanna Troughton, Blackie
The Shepherd Boy, Kim Lewis, Walker Books
Antarctica, Helen Cowcher, André Deutsch
Dr Xargle's Book of Earth Tiggers, Jeanne Willis, Andersen Press
The Hefty Fairy, Nicholas Allan, Hutchinson
Lost, Tony Kerins, J.M. Dent
The Mystery of the Blue Arrows, David and Chuck McKee, Andersen Press

Brave Babette and Sly Tom, Elzbieta, Faber
The Snowman, Raymond Briggs, Penguin
The Mousehole Cat, Antonia Barber, Walker
Pear Tree Farm, Colin and Moira Maclean, Kingfisher
Bear's Adventure, Benedict Blathwayt, Walker Books
Bringing the Rain to Kapiti Plain, Verna Aardema, Macmillan
Odette, Kay Fender, Gollancz
The Jolly Postman, Janet Ahlberg, Heinemann
The Turtle and the Island, Barbara Ker Wilson and Frane Lessac, Frances Lincoln Ltd
The Playground, Diane Wilmer, Collins
The Worm Book, Janet and Allan Ahlberg, Armada
Feelings, Aliki, Pan Books
The Farmyard Cat, Christine Anello and Sharon Thompson, Hodder & Stoughton
Amoko and Efua Bear, Sonia Appiah, Deutsch
Ollie Forgot, Tedd Arnold, Heinemann
The Sandal, Tony Bradman, Andersen Press
Have You Seen My Cat?, Eric Carle, Hodder & Stoughton
Go Away, William, Margaret Carter and Carol Wright, Hodder & Stoughton
The Day of the Rainbow, Ruth Craft, Heinemann
The Weather Cat, Helen Cresswell, Collins
At the Café Splendid, Terry Denton, Oxford University Press
Charles Tiger, Siobhan Dodds, Armada
The Singing Sack, Helen East, A. & C. Black
Sid the Kitten, Mark Foreman, Andersen Press
Tom's Pocket, Sarah Garland, Reinhardt/Viking Kestrel
Wayne Hoskins and the Pram Lady, Jennifer Gubb, Meridor Books
Peedie Peebles' Summer/Winter Book, Mairi Hedderwick, Bodley Head
Sebastian: The Tale of a Curious Kitten, Vanessa Julian-Ottie, Heinemann
Geraldine's Big Show, Holly Keller, Julia MacRae
Lily Takes a Walk, Satoshi Kitamura, Blackie
UFO Diary, Satoshi Kitamura, Andersen Press
Tenrec's Twigs, Bert Kitchen, Lutterworth
Come Back, Hercules, Rob Lewis, Macdonald
Six Crows, Leo Lionni, Andersen Press
Albert and Albertine at the Seaside, Moira and Colin Maclean, Hutchinson
Katie's Picture Show, James Mayhew, Orchard
Farm Noises, Jane Miller, Dent
Rex – The Most Special Car in the World, Victor Osborne, Dent
We're Going on a Bear Hunt, Michael Rosen, Walker Books
Where Do the Wicked Witches Live?, Juliet and Charles Snape, Picture Corgi
Brave Irene, William Steig, Gollancz
Sophie's Bucket, Catherine Stock, Methuen

Spots, Feathers and Curly Tails, Nancy Tafuri, Julia MacRae
The Sandhorse, Ann Turnbull, Andersen Press
Great Gran Gorilla and the Robbers, Martin Waddell, Walker Books
The Park in the Dark, Martin Waddell, Walker Books
Casper's Walk, Cindy Ward, Macdonald
Max's Chocolate Chicken, Rosemary Wells, Collins
Teddy Bear Boatman, Phoebe and Joan Worthington, Penguin
Snappity Snap, Stephen Wyllie and Maureen Roffey, Macmillan
The Shell Dragon, Lynn Zirkel, Oxford University Press
Something is Going to Happen, Charlotte Zolotow, Collins

NURSERY RHYMES AS STARTING POINTS

Mary had a Little Lamb, Jack and Jill Went Up the Hill, The Grand Old Duke of York and Hickory Dickory Dock are all excellent starting points for introducing vocabulary relating to direction and movement. Classroom friezes could be made depicting the stories in the rhymes, annotated by appropriate words such as 'up', 'down' and 'hill'.

Dr Foster Went to Gloucester and Incey Wincey Spider can be used as the basis for discussion of concepts relating to water and the weather.

There Was an Old Woman, Baa Baa Black Sheep and Jack and Jill Went Up the Hill can be related to the origins and use of resources, and aspects of human geography.

COMPUTER PROGRAMS

Relating to geographical skills

Dread Dragon Droom
Pip's Island Adventure
Fun School – Mazes
Magnetic Mazes
Infant General – suitable program on this disk
Pictogram – Colette Rose (CECC)
Viewpoints – A300 – Sherston
Tiny Logo
Honeypot

Relating to places

Concept Keyboard
    The Police
    The Farm

The Park
and any that you produce yourself.
My World
Our World
Church Street (Touch Explorer +)
The Village (Genesis)

Relating to physical geography

Use Touch Explorer – overlay of British Isles – identify various places
Genesis

Relating to human geography

Fun School 2 – shopping program.

ATLASES – SUITABLE FOR KEY STAGE 1

Brimax Books, *My First Atlas* (1989)
Dorling Kindersley, *The Picture Atlas of the World* (1992)
Hamlyn, *Children's Atlas of the World* (1987)
Hamlyn, *Deans Junior Picture Atlas* (1989)
Kingfisher Books, *Pictorial Atlas* (1991)
Schofield and Sims, *A First Atlas of the World* (1991)
Usborne Publishing, *The Usborne Picture Atlas* (1986)
Usborne Publishing, *The Usborne Children's Atlas of the World* (1979)
World International Publishing, *My First Atlas* (1991)

USEFUL ADDRESSES

Ordnance Survey maps, available from:

Cook, Hammond & Kell Ltd
The London Map Centre
22–24 Caxton Street
London SW1 0QU

The Goad Map Shop
Chas E Goad Ltd
8–12 Salisbury Square
Old Hatfield
Hertfordshire HL9 5BR

Trade Relations (Sales Division)
Ordnance Survey
Romsey Road
Maybush
Southampton SO9 4DH

Aerial Photographs, available from:
Aerial Photography Unit (MAFF)
Cambridge

Aerofilms
Gate Studios
Station Road
Borehamwood
Hertfordshire WD6 1EJ
Will take aerial photographs to order and have a library of photographs available.

Geonex UK Ltd
92–94 Church Road
Mitcham
Surrey CR4 3RD
Can supply photographs of any school site in the UK and produces a pack for sale entitled *Discovering Aerial Photographs*. Further details are available from their education officer.

Photo Air
Photo Air House
191A Main Street
Yaxley
Peterborough PE7 3LD
Have a wide range of aerial photographs in stock and can only deal with specific individual orders.

PROFESSIONAL ASSOCIATIONS

Readers are encouraged to subscribe to two professional associations which publish journals containing a wealth of practical guidance for primary teachers, including material relevant to teaching and learning in the first three years of school. Both also produce a range of other publications. Further details are available from their national headquarters:

The Geographical Association (primary membership)
343 Fulwood Road
Sheffield S10 3BP
(Journal: *Primary Geographer*)

The National Association for Environmental Education
University of Wolverhampton
The Gorway
Walsall
Staffordshire WS1 3BD
(Journal: *Environmental Education*)

Postscript

It is hoped that this book has shown how building upon first-hand experiences, practical investigations and interactions with the natural and built environments, and helping children to begin to appreciate the complex interrelationships between people, culture and biophysical surroundings are essential starting points for teaching and learning in geography and environmental education. Indeed, the most valuable and readily available resource is the environment itself. Young children are fascinated by their surroundings and have a tremendous capacity to build upon natural learning experiences that take place within them. A wealth of secondary resource material – books, audio- and video-tapes, television programmes, archives, maps, illustrative material, poems and plays about the world, about people and environmental issues and interrelationships – is not just desirable but an essential focus of successful classroom work. These will combine with experiences derived from the environment itself to ensure progress in, and give structure and meaning to learning tasks.

If a primary school's co-ordinated approach to the inclusion of geography and environmental education is to be successful, it depends as much upon the attitude of those designing and implementing it as on the content of what is being taught and learnt. The importance of developing pupils' attitudes has been discussed, but the critical importance of educators' attitudes has so far escaped attention. Central to geography and the study of the environment is the importance of attitudes and values, especially if a fundamental aim is to change people's attitudes from exploitation and dominance to global protection and care. This is, of course, a deeply personal issue and every individual has to be responsible for his or her own attitude changes and concern for future generations. Nevertheless, the teacher's role cannot be overemphasised. If a real impact is to be made, environmental awareness in the school as a whole is surely essential. In part this involves the successful implementation of programmes of work and progressive topics of a geographical and environmental nature, incorporating those components which this book has highlighted. It also takes account of the *whole* school environment, its ethos, its approach to caring for people and other living things, and, of course, the overall personal development of each child as an individual.

This book opened with some comments from young learners. It will conclude with some of the thoughts of Nicola, aged 4, from Stanford, California:

Nicola	I'm going to tell you something that's very awful – we are trying to save trees . . . they're trying to chop down the trees in this beautiful place, but you know what, we're trying and trying to save them from not being chopped down . . . but they're sick, but we're trying to save them even though they're sick.
Researcher	I'm so pleased you're trying to save them. Who told you about them?
Nicola	My dad . . . my mommy, I meant.
Researcher	Right. So some people really try to spoil our world, but we can help to take care of it. Can you think of any ways that you and I can help to take care of our world, and help to keep it beautiful?
Nicola	Not to chop down the trees . . . and my grandma always does . . . um . . . if someone throws litter around, you want to know what she does? She picks them up.
Researcher	And what's the right thing to do with litter?
Nicola	Keep them until you put it in the trash can. That's what I do.
Researcher	That's right – and, do you know, sometimes litter can get used again . . .
Nicola	Uh-huh.
Researcher	Do you know what we call that? When waste . . . garbage gets used again?
Nicola	Recycling.
Researcher	Well done, Nicky.
Nicola	Do you know why I know? The um . . . trash can up there says recycle. I even saw it on this programme . . . that's . . . um . . . recycle. And I even saw how you can do other things . . . um . . . with trees on the programme.
Researcher	Well, that's very good. Do you know why we must recycle?
Nicola	Yes. To make new things and . . . um . . . save the bad . . . em, not . . . um . . . save the used things.
Researcher	Right – so we can use used things to make new things. And that's important for our world.
Nicola	I know.
Researcher	What are we saving if we use things over and over again?
Nicola	Um . . . saving trees.

Researcher	Right. And do you always recycle your things – your family recycles?
Nicola	Uh-huh. We used to recycle these little glass bottles me and my brother used to use. And now we don't use them any more, but my brother still uses a bottle . . . and it's a different kind of these plastic ones.
Researcher	Well, Nicky, you told me you were smart, and you are right. You know a lot about these things, so you understand that our world is very beautiful, and we need to take care of it.
Nicola	Mmm.
Researcher	Why do you think you really want to take special care of the world?
Nicola	Because I love this world, even though it gets too cold in the winter.
Researcher	Why do you love the world? What's really special about it?
Nicola	Um . . . that it's . . . that it . . . gets to be warmer as the year comes, and it gets to be colder as the year comes.
Researcher	Right. Why is our world . . . why do you love it?
Nicola	Because it's so beautiful and the leaves turn to colours . . . and in the summer . . .

No child in school is too young to begin to stand in awe of the world and to reflect upon the glories of the natural environment and the achievements of human life, or to take those first steps along the path towards individual concern, responsibility and action.

References

Acredolo, L.P., Pick, H.L. and Olson, M.G. (1975) Environmental differentiation and familiarity as determinants of children's memory for spatial location. *Developmental Psychology* II, 495–501.

Appleyard, D. (1970) Styles and methods of structuring a city. *Environment and Behavior* 2, 101–117.

Atkins, C.L. (1981) Introducing basic map and globe concepts to young children. *Journal of Geography* 80, 228–233.

Bell, P.A., Fisher, J.D., Baum, A. and Greene, T.C. (1990) *Environmental Psychology.* Fort Worth: Holt, Rinehart & Winston Inc.

Blades, M. and Spencer, C. (1986) Map use in the environment and educating children to use maps. *Environmental Education and Information* 5, 187–204.

Blades, M. and Spencer, C. (1987a) Young children's recognition of environmental features from aerial photographs and maps. *Environmental Education and Information* 6, 189–198.

Blades, M. and Spencer, C. (1987b) The use of maps by 4–6 year old children in a large-scale maze. *British Journal of Developmental Psychology* 5, 19–24.

Bluestein, N. and Acredolo, L.P. (1979) Developmental changes in map reading skills. *Child Development* 50, 691–697.

Boardman, D.J. (1983) *Graphicacy and Geography Teaching.* Beckenham: Croom Helm.

Carpenter, T.P., Moser, J.M. and Romberg, T.A. (1982) *Addition and Subtraction: A Cognitive Perspective.* Hillsdale, NJ: Lawrence Erlbaum.

Catling, S. (1978) Cognitive mapping exercises as a primary geographical experience. *Teaching Geography* 3, 120–123.

Catling, S. (1988) Using maps and aerial photographs. In D. Mills (ed.) *Geographical Work in Primary and Middle School.* Sheffield: The Geographical Association.

Clark, M. (1976) *Young Fluent Readers.* London: Heinemann.

Cornell, E.H. and Hay, D.H. (1984) Children's acquisition of a route via different media. *Environment and Behavior* 16, 627–641.

Cornell, E.H. and Heth, C.D. (1983) Spatial cognition: gathering strategies used by pre-school children. *Journal of Experimental Child Psychology* 35, 93–110.

Cousins, J.H., Siegel, A.W. and Maxwell, S.E. (1983) Way finding and cognitive mapping in large-scale environments. A test of a developmental model. *Journal of Experimental Child Psychology* 35, 1–20.

Darvizeh, Z. and Spencer, C.P. (1984) How do young children learn novel routes? The importance of landmarks in the child's retracing of routes through the large-scale environment. *Environmental Education and Information* 3, 97–105.

Department of Education and Science (DES) (1989) *Aspects of the Primary Curriculum. The Teaching and Learning of History and Geography.* London: HMSO.

DES/Welsh Office (1989) *Discipline in Schools*. London: HMSO.

DES (1991) *Geography in the National Curriculum*. London: HMSO.

Desforges, C. (1989) Understanding learning for teaching. *Westminster Studies in Education*. Vol. 12.

Devlin, A.S. (1976) The small-town cognitive map: adjusting to a new environment. In G.T. Moore and R.G. Golledge (eds) *Environmental Knowing*. Stroudsburg, PA: Dowden, Hutchinson & Ross.

Evans, G.W. (1980) Environmental cognition. *Psychological Bulletin* 88, 259–287.

Garling, T., Book, A. and Ergezen, N. (1982) Memory for the spatial layout of the everyday physical environment. *Scandinavian Journal of Psychology* 23, 23–35.

Garling, T., Book, A. and Lindberg, E. (1984) Cognitive-mapping of large-scale environments: the inter-relationship between action plans, acquisition and orientation. *Environment and Behavior* 16, 3–34.

Gellman, R. and Gallistel, C.R. (1978) *The Child's Understanding of Number*. Cambridge, MA: Harvard University Press.

Hall, N. (1987) *The Emergence of Literacy*. London: Hodder & Stoughton.

Hart, R. and Chawla, L. (1981) The development of children's concern for the environment. *Zeitschrift für Umweltpolitik* 4, 271–294.

Hart, R.A. and Moore, G.T. (1973) The development of spatial cognition: a review. In R.M. Downs and D. Stea (eds) *Image and Environment: Cognitive Mapping and Spatial Behavior*. Chicago: Aldine.

Hughes, M. (1986) *Children and Number*. London: Blackwell.

Jaspars, J., Van der Geer, J., Tajfel, H. and Johnson, N.B. (1963) On the development of national attitudes in children. *European Journal of Social Psychology* 2, 347–369.

Laurendeau, M. and Pinard, A. (1962) *Causal Thinking in the Child*. New York: New York International Universities Press.

Mills, D. (ed.) (1986) *Geographical Work in Primary and Middle Schools*. Sheffield: The Geographical Association. (Second edition)

Muir, M.E. and Blaut, J.M. (1969) The use of aerial photographs in teaching mapping to children in the first grade: an experimental study. In D. Stea (ed.) *Place Perception Research Reports* 2, Worcester, MA: Graduate School of Geography.

National Curriculum Council (1990a) *Curriculum Guidance 3: The Whole Curriculum*, York: NCC.

National Curriculum Council (1990b) *Curriculum Guidance 7: Environmental Education*, York: NCC.

National Curriculum Council (1991) *Geography: Non-Statutory Guidance*. York: NCC.

Ofsted (1993) *Geography Key Stages 1, 2, 3 First Year. The Implementation of the Curriculum Requirements of the Education Reform Act*. London: HMSO.

Palmer, J.A. (1992a) Life experiences of environmental educators. *Environmental Education*. Winter.

Palmer, J.A. (1992b) Digest of research paper: development of concern for the environment. Vol. 1–3 Autumn. *Primary Life*. Oxford: Blackwell.

Palmer, J.A. (1993) From Santa Claus to sustainability: emergent understanding of concepts and issues in Environmental Science. *International Journal of Science Education* 15(5), 487–496.

Piaget, J. (1954) *The Construction of Reality in the Child*. New York: Basic Books. (Original edition, 1937)

Piaget, J. (1960a) *Judgement and Reasoning in the Child*. New York: Harcourt & Brace. (Original edition, 1928)

Piaget, J. (1960b) *The Child's Conception of Physical Causality*. Totowa, NJ: Littlefield, Adams, Patterson. (Original edition, 1927)

Piaget, J. and Inhelder, B. (1956) *The Child's Conception of Space*. London: Routledge & Kegan Paul.

Piaget, J. and Inhelder, B. (1967) *The Child's Conception of Space* New York: Norton.

Piaget, J., Inhelder, B. and Szeminska, A. (1960) *The Child's Conception of Geometry*. London: Routledge & Kegan Paul.

Piché, D. (1981) The spontaneous geography of the urban child. In D.T. Herbert and R.J. Johnson (eds) *Geography and the Urban Environment: Progress in Research and Applications* Vol. 4. Chichester: John Wiley.

Pick, H.L. and Lockman, J.J. (1981) From frames of reference to spatial representations. In L.S. Liben, A.H. Patterson and N. Newcombe (eds) *The Life Span*. New York: Academic Press.

Siegel, A. and White, S. (1975) The development of spatial representations of large-scale environments. In H.W. Reese (ed.) *Advances in Child Development and Behaviour* 12, 167–182.

Somerville, S.C. and Bryant, P.E. (1985) Young children's use of spatial co-ordinates. *Child Development* 56, 604–613.

Spencer, C., Blades, M. and Morsley, K. (1989) *The Child in the Physical Environment*. Chichester: John Wiley & Sons.

Stillwell, R. and Spencer, C. (1974) Children's early preferences for other nations and their subsequent acquisition of knowledge about those nations. *European Journal of Social Psychology* 3, 345–349.

Storm, M. (1984) Teaching about minorities. In N. Fyson (ed.) *The Development Puzzle*. Sevenoaks: Hodder & Stoughton/CWDE.

Tajfel, H. (1981) *Human Groups and Social Categories*. Cambridge: Cambridge University Press.

Tajfel, H. and Jahoda, G. (1966) Development in children of concepts and attitudes about their own and other countries. *Proceedings of the 18th International Congress of Psychology*, Moscow.

Vygotsky, L.S. (1979) *Mind and Society*. Cambridge, MA: Harvard University Press.

Welsh, R.L. and Blasch, B.B. (eds) (1980) *Foundations of Orientation and Mobility*. New York: American Foundation for the Blind.

Name index

Subject index